PSYCHOPATH:

Manipulation, Con Men

And

Relationship Fraud

3rd Edition

Jeffery Dawson

reliable complete information. No warranties of any kind are expressed or implied. Readers acknowledge that the author is not engaging in the rendering of legal, financial or professional advice.

By reading this document, the reader agrees that under no circumstances are we responsible for any losses, direct or indirect, which are incurred as a result of the use of information contained within this document, including, but not limited to, —errors, omissions, or inaccuracies.

Table of Contents

INTRODUCTION

Popular culture has led us to believe that the psychopath is primarily a criminal – a serial killer, or perhaps a recidivist bank robber or rapist. This stereotype, though, is only the tip of the psychopathic iceberg. Beneath the dark, cold waters lurks a much bigger story.

In fact, psychopaths only account for between 20% - 40% (estimates vary) of prison populations. It's much more likely we'll meet psychopaths walking down the street, or in front of us in the line at the supermarket.

Originally identified as a personality disorder in the 19th Century, psychopathy fascinates us all. In films like *Silence of the Lambs* or *We Need to Talk about Kevin,* the psychopath has moved on from its status as a mythical monster. Awareness that the psychopath may be next door, or even in our homes is growing. With the help of the internet and 24/7 news media, psychopathy has become a hot topic of conversation and clinical professionals are sharing that conversation.

Interestingly, there is no psychiatric or psychological organization that sanctions the diagnosis "psychopath". Because is it classified as a personality disorder, psychopathy has no actual diagnostic status in terms of classification.

Until 1950, the term was used to describe what become known as psychopathic or sociopathic personality, as the clinical community's understanding of psychopathy grew. The disorder is now most commonly known as Anti-social Personality Disorder (APD). For the purposes of this book, though, we will use the word most popularly associated with the disorder for clarity.

Psychopaths exist in every area of life and every conceivable profession (although it's true they tend to gravitate toward those professions which afford them power, privilege and financial gain). These professions are some of the most respected in the world. Chief Executive Officers, surgeons, police officers – all these professional groups harbor psychopaths in their midst.

There is some disagreement in the clinical community concerning the difference between psychopathy and sociopathy which should be discussed at the outset. Some clinicians make no distinction between the two. Others claim some fine distinctions.

For example, while impulsivity is a shared trait of the (arguably) two disorders, sociopaths engage in this trait more erratically. They lack the calculating, systematic approach employed by psychopaths. Further, there are clear indicators that sociopathy is entirely generated environmentally (nurture) and is not inherent (nature) to the subject. With psychopaths, there are specific genetic factors at work, as well as brain irregularities and chemical imbalances that point clearly to nature as the primary cause of the disorder.

Sociopathy and psychopathy, though, are almost indistinguishable in terms of traits and manifestations of those traits. For that reason, this book will discuss psychopathy as a blanket term encompassing both clinical categories.

It's also a generally accepted principal that most psychopaths are male. The proportion of male to female psychopaths has, in fact, between estimated to be as high as 20:1.

Recent research, however, indicates that this may not be entirely true. In 2012, the study identified Borderline Personality Disorder as a phenotypic (to "show type", primarily by examination of characteristics) expression of psychopathy. This finding challenged earlier understandings concerning sex and psychopathy (see case study #3 in the chapter, Case Studies).

The study's findings suggest that psychopathy in women is closely associated with Borderline Personality Disorder, not as a co-morbidity, but as a condition which has significantly muddied the diagnostic waters in confrontation of women with psychopathy. In short, women psychopaths may express symptoms and traits differently than men, while having the same or very similar psychopathic traits.

Often, though, a BPL diagnosis is arrived at with female subjects, regardless of the fact that many of these women display symptoms and traits consistent with those of psychopathy.

Overall, research into psychopathy in women is hampered by the assumption that the condition is primarily a "boy's club". Another study, Psychopathy in Women: theoretical and clinical perspectives has identified important differences between manifestation of traits in women and men. Criminal behavior, in particular, was more readily modeled in males than in females.

Despite recent challenges to the almost globally accepted belief that psychopathy is more common in men than women, this belief continues to prevail. For that reason, the masculine article is used throughout this book.

Contact with a psychopath can be disorienting. In the initial stages of contact, psychopaths may seem charming and amiable. Their verbal and communicative skills leave those they engage impressed and disarmed. These skills are the psychopath's most valuable tool. Coupled with the ability to present in a manner which is pleasing to many people in terms of social aptitude and aesthetic appeal, the psychopath uses "mimicry" (the act of producing a facsimile or copy) in order to blend in with other people.

Psychopaths lack affective ability. They do not experience the emotional life of a normal human being. For that reason, when they laugh, smile, express sadness or any other emotion, they are not genuinely experiencing it. They are mimicking it based on their observations of other people expressing it.

Psychopaths learn, through intent observation of other people, that feigning emotion is expected of them and so they do it in order to blend in. Their knowledge of the emotional lives of non-psychopaths enables them to get close to other people, to insinuate themselves into social and business circles and to enjoy the breadth of human relationships.

Psychopaths, though, have no need of such relationships on an emotional level. For the rest of us, it's very difficult to understand why they would pursue them, if this were the case. But without them, how would a psychopath inflict the kind of damage they do on others? How would they draw near to a lover, a friend, a business associate, or a teacher?

It would be virtually impossible.

Therefore, the very first thing to be considered is the reality that psychopaths are difficult to spot. Even when they begin their manipulative dance, they can elude detection. Too often, their dance partners are unaware of psychopathic traits and the *modus operandi* (methodology) being employed.

Those the psychopath targets for their very special and very sophisticated brand of abuse will, even if aware that something is wrong, or that they're being abused, deny what's happening, in almost every instance. They will turn the red flag moments over in their minds and come to the conclusion that they're terribly mistaken. Even when friends, family and colleagues come to them with concerns about the psychopath in question, they'll shrug off their objections and keep right on dancing.

That's because the psychopath has, with calculated focus, ensnared the target to the point that reality has become skewed and distorted. Having constructed a complex identity in the eyes of the target, the psychopath is inviolable. The psychopath's ability to erect an elaborate façade of not only normalcy, but also social aptitude and charm, creates trust in targets and impunity for the psychopath and his actions.

Psychopaths work over time to convince their targets both that they believe the target to be incredibly special and they, themselves, are incredibly special. Having gained the complete trust of their targets, psychopaths immunize themselves against external criticism, often isolating their victims from those who may see through them.

Once the psychopath becomes bored, the dance will abruptly end. The psychopath's dance partner will be unceremoniously dumped on the dance floor, as our hero traipses off into the distance, unencumbered by remorse or self-examination of any kind. Gone will be the dance partner's self-respect, emotional security and quite probably, financial well being.

Typically, psychopaths engage in a pattern of three clearly defined stages in their relationships with targets. These are:

Assessment – choosing the target, according to non-verbal, followed by verbal cues.

Manipulation – manipulation to achieve power and domination over the chosen target, through deceit, gas lighting (causing targets to question their state of mental health by presenting untruths as fact, particularly with regard to past events and the target's character).

Abandonment – removing themselves from the target/predator relationship suddenly, due to boredom, the threat of discovery by an outside party, or revelation of wrongdoing.

Ultimately the targets of psychopaths blame themselves for having allowed the psychopath anywhere near them. Used, confused and abused, the abandoned target sits among the wreckage left by the predator in a toxic stew of self-loathing and depression.

Even though it's true psychopaths prey on targets with particular traits (sometimes acquired via serial contact in previous relationships with similarly disordered partners), they can never be blamed. No one deserves to be targeted for manipulation. No one deserves to have his or her life turned upside down and no one deserves to be robbed, spiritually or financially by a predator with a severe personality disorder.

The best thing anyone can do is educate themselves about psychopathy. This is the most effective defense against waking up in the ruins of a once happy, successful life. Knowing the traits of a psychopath, recognizing and naming them before arriving at the unfortunate status of "target", is an invaluable tool for everyone to have.

Because psychopaths can appear, at first glance, to be so innocuous, it's extraordinarily easy to fall into the hellish rabbit hole of victimhood. It needn't happen.

This brief introduction will elaborated on at length in this book. We hope you'll find here weapons for your arsenal against the psychopaths in our midst. If you're already doing battle with a life partner, friend, colleague or even a child, we hope the contents of this book will help you find a means of coping with the situation and managing the effects of psychopathy on your life.

It should be made clear at this point that all personality disorders don't cause the kind of chaos psychopathy is capable of. Psychopathy is a virulent pathology that turns worlds upside down, destroying relationships in the workplace and at home. It ruins friendships.

It's estimated that approximately 1% of the general population fits the diagnostic criteria for Anti-Social Personality Disorder (as defined by the Psychopathy Checklist, developed by Canadian psychologist Robert D. Hare, in the 1970s). While this might not sound like a lot of people, think about it. If there are almost seven billion people on the planet, that means there are approximately 70,000,000 psychopaths in the world today.

That's a distressing number.

Psychopathy impacts society at every level from the home, to the workplace, to corporate and political leadership. In fact, psychopaths are found in every walk of life. They're your neighbors, friends and co-workers. They're even your family.

This book will explore the symptoms and traits of

psychopathy, what's known about the condition and how this illness affects the world we live in. It will explore diagnostic tools, strategies for dealing with a psychopath and how to recognize one in daily life.

Forewarned is forearmed, so this informational book is intended to provide readers with the tools to see a psychopath coming, understand the nature of the disorder and to take action before becoming a target. It may also prove of value for those who suspect that a loved one, co-worker or acquaintance is a psychopath.

Unless the reader is a clinical professional (psychologist, family doctor, psychiatrist, pediatrician, etc.), you are not equipped or licensed to make a diagnosis in the event you suspect someone around you of being a psychopath. Should this be the case, it's of utmost importance that you resort to a professional or professionals for assistance.

Before we delve into the world of psychopaths, though, it's important to define a number of other conditions that bear some resemblance to psychopathy and even share some of its traits. It's also important to define some general terms in order to fully, and as accurately as possible, explore the world of the psychopath.

A basic knowledge of the diagnostic criteria and traits of personality disorders can also provide us with insights into our own behavior. While this book is not written by a clinical professional, care has been taken to present the information herein as accurately as possible. Information is powerful and we hope to provide you with some of the best and most up-to-date available.

Extreme conditions (like psychopathy) require professional intervention. Many of the conditions described herein, though, are treatable with awareness and expert guidance. Guidance and information are main intentions of this book – to raise awareness about these disorders toward greater understanding.

CHAPTER 1: WHAT IS A PERSONALITY?

Human personality is actually a confluence of our thoughts, feelings and behavior patterns. The perception we have of ourselves and the way we understand and relate to the outside world molds our personality.

> ➤ Personality is a pattern of relatively permanent traits and unique characteristics that give both consistency and individuality to a person's behavior.

> ➤ Personality is a combination of all the intrinsic qualities and characteristics of a person that influences the behavior, traits and habits of a person.

In short, personality is the human sum of all we are to the world we live in. Our genes, our family backgrounds and our experiences combine to create personality – our unique way of being in the world.

Factors That Make an Impact on our Personality

We develop unique personality traits during childhood, but there are two other factors to be considered in its formation.

Our genes: We inherit certain character or personality traits from our parents and these are part of our temperament. We call these factors "*nature*".

Our environment: The background we grow up in, the memorable (bad or good) events that occurred in that setting, our relationships with family members and other members of our society are all formative. We call these factors "*nurture*".

If the combination of these factors is healthy, we may lead normal, healthy lives and enjoy strong and healthy relationships with the people around us. It's possible that our genetic composition makes us more or less vulnerable to developing a personality disorder, but extremely stressful situations in our life can serve as triggers. In the case of psychopathy, there is a heavy genetic influence, coupled with a probability of brain abnormalities.

There is a great deal of debate in the scientific community about the respective roles of nature and nurture and their combined influences. The debate centers on the proportion of influence of the two. Which might be more readily assigned culpability in the development of personality disorders and human personality, in general?

Professor Danielle Posthuma, a statistical geneticist at Vrie Universiteit Amsterdam, was a research participant in a recent study, pitting the two influences against one another. The study concluded that nature and nurture were in a virtual dead heat in terms of which was more influential in the development of a non-pathological human personality.

The study (published May 15, 2015 in the journal, Nature Genetics) surveyed the results of research into similar data concerning twins. Fully 2,748 studies were consulted, conducted over 50 years, between 1958 and 2012. 17,000 traits were examined, in total.

It was determined that nature accounted for 49% of developmental outcomes, while nurture accounted for 51% of it. Interestingly, it was found that Anti-Social Personality Disorder (psychopathy) and autism were more likely to be influenced by genetics (nature) than environmental factors (nurture).

Personality disorders all have one thing in common – they can be disruptive and create chaos in the conduct of daily life for all concerned, including the person with the condition. A personality disorder can clearly be identified when the behavior of the person interferes with the ability to interact with others in normative ways and thus, life in general.

People with personality disorders have strained relationships with family members, with colleagues, or with their schoolmates. Sometimes they prefer leading socially isolated lives or may resort to substance abuse as a form of self-medication.

Many of the conditions described in this book are misunderstood and very often, undiagnosed in those who suffer from them. The stigma still (in this day and age) associated with mental illness can prevent patients from seeking a diagnosis. Coupled with the reluctance of prospective patients to seek diagnosis, because of that stigma are two presenting issues that represent roadblocks to extending treatment to those who suffer with these conditions. Another is the patient's lack of self-awareness concerning his behavior. Add to this the reluctance of friends, families and co-workers to confront people suffering with psychopathy and other personality disorders about their symptoms and urging them to seek a diagnosis and eventual treatment.

It's not the easiest subject to broach.

Please note that in the case of all conditions detailed, within their respective "clusters" (categories), many symptoms overlap their fellows in the cluster (please see the chapter on Personality Disorders). Only with the assistance of a clinical professional is it possible to discern which of the disorders is actually in play. Diagnosing others and self-diagnosis are strongly discouraged.

CHAPTER 2: WHAT IS A PERSONALITY DISORDER?

A person with a personality disorder is often unable to express himself normally. Perhaps the personality has been so deeply affected by certain life events that he becomes dysfunctional. Perhaps the genetic makeup of the person has skewed personality toward that dysfunction, or injury to the brain has occurred (particularly in the case of psychopathy). The behavior of a person with a personality disorder can be disruptive for those around him, negatively impacting the conduct of daily life.

Unusual patterns of behavior, thought and function are common across the spectrum of personality disorders. These can be confusing for those interacting with the person in question, or even intimidating. People with personality disorders find it difficult to function adequately in any number of social, professional or domestic situations. Their perceptions of the world diverge from what is considered normative by most people and may be delusional or distorted.

Many people with personality disorders have not been diagnosed and may be completely unaware there's anything wrong. A lack of self-awareness prevents seeking a diagnosis, because people with these disorders may honestly believe there's nothing to diagnose. Too often, family, friends and co-workers are reluctant to broach the subject, due to the stigma associated with mental illness and personality disorders, particular. Nobody wants to be the person who says, "Houston, we have a problem!"

People with personality disorders can live with the illness completely undetected for many years due to this reluctance, never knowing why things in their lives so often seem to go "sideways". Why do they have such difficulty retaining employment, or maintaining relationships (like friendships or romantic relationships)? If only someone around them knew what to look for, these people might be given the opportunity to seek professional help and move on with their lives.

Causes of Personality Disorders:

As discussed above, research is finding that nature and nurture seem to weigh in equally when it comes to the source of personality disorders. Each individual being treated for a disorder will have a different story. Genetics, environmental and social realities as well as the possibility of early childhood trauma must be explored to determine causal links.

Family circumstances and resulting trauma:

While the APA describes trauma as "an emotional response to a terrible event, like an accident, rape, or natural disaster", psychological trauma theorist, Dr. Peter Levine defines it in terms of the response to and symptoms displayed by the individual undergoing experiences of this type. Trauma of all kinds can evoke a variety of symptoms in those who experience it, including anxiety, denial, shock, disbelief, anger, irritability, mood swings, guilt, shame, self-blame, hopelessness and sadness.

There is limited evidence to suggest that disturbed family circumstances contribute to the development of personality disorders. However, in some cases there is a pattern. Some children living in unhealthy family situations develop personality disorders as a result.

It's estimated that 10% of criminal offenders witnessed domestic violence in the home as juveniles (Nanning Pilot Anti-Violence project, China). The American Psychological Institute (APD) reports that a link has been found between Borderline Personality Disorder, as well as Schizotypal, Obsessive Compulsive and Avoidant types and witnessing domestic violence. All people with these personality disorders were found to be more likely to have suffered sexual abuse as children. People with these personality disorders were also found to suffer from Post Traumatic Stress Disorder (PTSD) as a co-morbidity (attendant disorder), in the instance of childhood sexual abuse.

The APD also states that one healthy relationship in the family can serve to mitigate the effects of the abuse described. A relationship with a friend or teaching professional can also be the foundation of a child in this situation developing without the encumbrance of a personality disorder.

Other trauma – war/genocide:

The effect of war on the psychological health of children and the outfall as they grow into adults is a developing area of study. In a world consumed by civil unrest and war, the damage done to the development of children in war torn areas is a matter for urgent assessment, toward the stability of the global community.

In Gaza the continuing war occasioned by a combination of guerilla and state actions against civilian populations has resulted in untold trauma on juveniles there. Medicins sans Frontiers reports that a third of patients seen in Gaza are under the age of 13 and that these patients have encountered violence as a way of life for as long as they can remember. The fact that they live in a state of "anxiety and terror" will have repercussions for the international community for decades (perhaps generations) to come.

Perhaps a fitting model for study in the area is Rwanda. In 1994, the Rwandan genocide was responsible for the deaths of 800,000 people in 100 days. All over the country, roaming vigilantes, wielding machetes, indiscriminately killed men, women and children. Children who are now adults, as well as child soldiers implicated in the genocide witnessed this relentless mayhem.

A study into the issue by Heide Rieder and Thomas Elbert compared the mental health of the children of survivors of the genocide against those of prisoners who had participated and were being held for trial. The study, which appeared in the journal, Conflict and Health in March 2013, discovered trans-generational damage occasioned by the violence in both participant and victim groups. Ultimately, these effects were seen to be more pronounced in the victim group (next generation). The study concludes, however, that the mental health of the entire community (in other words, not only the victims, but the participants) should be considered in order to adequately address the national, post-genocide trauma load.

These two examples provide sufficient bases for global attention to the effects of the communal trauma occasioned by war, genocide and other violent upheavals on children who witness them. The generational effect (the transference of the trauma load from the generation originally witnessing communal violence to the next) merits special attention. How will this generation respond when it ascends to adulthood? How will its trauma play out on the international stage and in the lives of those not only witness it, but their offspring?

Understanding that nurture shares primacy with nature in terms of influencing psychological outcomes in children is instructive and cautionary for the sake of the future.

Genetics and brain function:
As detailed above, genetics have recently been found to be the primary cause of psychopathy. While environmental factors may exacerbate or trigger symptoms, it's now clear that psychopathy is written into the personality of people with the disorder, through chemical and genetic factors.

Recent studies also suggest that damage to the brain may provoke symptoms associated with psychopathy. The journal Social Cognitive and Affective Neuro-Science published a study in 2007 which suggests that damage impacting brain functions may also give rise to psychopathy.

Entitled Selective Deficit in personal moral judgment following damage to the ventromedial prefrontal cortex was found to give rise to psychopathic traits. In this respect, the study's findings throw further light on the causes of the condition. These suggest that psychopaths may suffer from impairment in connectivity between the ventromedial prefrontal cortex (vmPFC) and the amygdala (which processes negative stimuli).

If this connection is, in fact, faulty in the brain of a psychopath, what it means is that the brain of the psychopath is unable to register an emotional response to fear, disapproval, sadness, or similar emotions as they're exhibited in other people. This would at least partially explain at least one symptom of psychopathy (lack of empathy).

A separate study, however, found that lesions on the brain also impact the psychopathic brain's ability to process negative stimuli. Entitled "Psychopaths know right from wrong, but don't care," the study appeared in the same journal cited above in 2010. Its findings suggest that lesions on the brain are at fault in the instance of the psychopath's inability to invest fear and pain reactions with any value. Lesions occurring in the vmPFC cause psychopaths to be blind to the unacceptable nature of moral and physical violations that would be recognized by subjects with healthy brains. Damage to this region of the brain (which governs introspection) resulted in subjects being unable to experience guilt or remorse.

CHAPTER 3: TYPES OF PERSONALITY DISORDERS

Based on the common characteristics and symptoms of these disorders, they are classified into three distinct groups. By reading through the symptoms, it will become clear why these groupings are configured, as they are – many of the symptoms for disorders within each cluster overlap.

Cluster A personality disorders:

People suffering with Cluster A disorders display distorted perception, abnormal emotional responses, extremes of impulse control (highs/lows) and interpersonal dysfunction.

Paranoid personality disorder:

Paranoid Personality Disorder sufferers model extreme suspicion of others. People with PPD are generally characterized by having a high degree of mistrust and very high levels of suspicion of others. This impacts their ability to relate to other people. PPD sufferers believe that everyone around them is motivated by ill will. Hence, they live each day suspecting everyone they encounter; their motives and intentions toward them.

Paranoia is a strong feeling of doubting the intentions and motives of others, with no basis for doing so. These baseless fears permeate and damage every aspect of the PPD sufferer's life, to the point of complete dysfunction. The film Conspiracy Theory *is a reasonable depiction of how PPD can impact the lives of those who have the disorder. Even the world around the PPD person can be perceived as rife with threat and danger.*

The disorder is found more in males than females and is known to begin manifesting in early adulthood.

Schizoid personality disorder:

Schizoid Personality Disorder is characterized by a pattern of considerable detachment from social relationships or involvement. A person with schizoid personality disorder finds it difficult to express emotion or might only do so in a very closed and restricted environment, thus communication with others is rather limited. This type of disorder is reasonably rare.

People with Schizoid Personality Disorder refrain from participating in social activities and shy away from interaction with others. Again, this type of disorder is more common in males than females.

A person with this disorder also lacks the skill to form close personal relationships and spends the majority of his or her time alone. Sometimes, individuals with Schizoid Personality Disorder may also find it difficult to express some of the most basic human emotions. For example, anger or even a response to a provocative situation would probably be problematic for a SPD sufferer.

SPD people often come across as emotionally flat; lacking in expression. They further lack life direction and consistently change or deviate from their goals and ambitions. Often, they find it difficult to respond or react to major life events, thus appearing to be inordinately passive.

Schizotypal personality disorder:

Persons with Schizotypal personality disorder model an acute deficit in normative behavior, thought and communication. This impacts interpersonal relationships and interactions. This disorder also affects speech, rendering it strikingly odd and idiosyncratic.

The Schizotypal person also rarely has command of more than a rudimentary vocabulary. Schizotypals often behave strangely; modelling distorted and disturbed thinking patterns. Intimacy, for schizotypals, is extremely uncomfortable and mostly avoided.

If schizotypals have any friends at all, these are very few in number. There is most probably only one primary relationship, as schizotypals are generally nervous when surrounded by strangers.

Schizotypals have a high inclination toward cults and often join them. This personality disorder can also give rise to high levels of depression and anxiety.

Cluster B personality disorders:

Cluster B disorders are typically characterized by histrionics (overwrought emotional responses) and emotional drama. They can be subdivided into four categories, as follows.

Antisocial personality disorder (aka psychopath):

Antisocial Personality Disorder is a chronic mental condition and is the personality disorder most closely associated with psychopathy. A person with APD thinks and perceives situations from a standpoint of complete emotional detachment, objectifying other people and viewing them as tools to be employed to achieve a specific, personal goal. APD people have no understanding that their actions are negative in the eyes of others and don't attach any value to such judgments. There is no accommodation for the consideration that other people are human beings with feelings, because (to be blunt) APD people do not have feelings. The psychopath is incapable of providing any accommodation to the feelings or rights of others, as they have no emotional or moral benchmark against which to measure these.

Psychopathic patterns of thinking and perception are highly destructive. People with APD lack any regard whatsoever for right and wrong and do not regard the feelings or wishes of others. APD types regard others as opportunities to be exploited and are entirely devoid of empathy. For reasons stated earlier (see section on genetics and brain function, and chapter on culpability) psychopaths are incapable of it.

APD affects more than one area of the sufferer's thinking, including cognitive ability, impulse control and interpersonal understanding/interaction. APD people's behavior tends to be inflexible, resulting in distressful social scenarios.

People with antisocial personality disorder often find themselves getting involved in legal issues. They have volatile and problematic relationships with the law, yet show no signs of remorse when confronted with any wrongdoing, believing themselves to be justified in their actions.

Highly manipulative, APD people are unwittingly rude and treat others with indifference and even contempt. Their facility for lying is viewed by them as allowable, due to the special status they confer upon themselves. They may also struggle with addictions to drugs or alcohol. Impulsive beyond any normal tendency to indulge in such unpredictable behavior, there is also a strong predilection to violence. Life's responsibilities (family, work, or other relationships) are seen by the APD person as inapplicable to them; inconvenient and without value.

As stated in the opening paragraph of this section, APD is considered to be the diagnostic home of psychopathy.

Borderline personality disorder:

Borderline Personality Disorder (BPD) is a serious mental illness and is often misunderstood. People with BPD have unstable moods, interpersonal relationships, a mutable self-image and equally mercurial behavior.

Prone to "cutting" (self-injury) and extreme impulsivity, BPD tends to occur in young adults (especially women) with psychological frameworks still in development and thus, vulnerable. BPD people also struggle with fear of abandonment and inappropriate anger. Showing up late for an appointment with a BPD friend can result in and out-of-proportion emotional response. Tardiness, to the BPD person is a form of abandonment and gives immediate rise to fears that he/she is about to be abandoned.

A high level of instability penetrates every sphere the BPD person's life. Work, family, individual self-worth and identity are all affected. Many other disorders may also be co-morbid in people with this disorder. The borderline personality disorder sufferer experiences anxiety, depression, eating disorders, substance and self-abuse and even suicides.

People may interpret the BPD person's character as "shallow", in order to account for the behaviors described.

Histrionic personality disorder:

People with Histrionic Personality Disorder show excessively emotional behavior and volatility. They have a tendency to regard everything in an inappropriately dramatic manner and habitually (almost obsessively) seek attention.

People with this disorder feel extremely uncomfortable and unappreciated if they are not the center of attention. There is a wide range of behavior patterns exhibited by people with this disorder, including the constant seeking of approval and attention, dramatization, overwhelming self-obsession and the employment of superficial flirtation and feigned seduction for the sake of getting attention. These last behaviors are often deployed in inappropriate social contexts.

At first glance, HPD people appear engaging and charming and are thus able to draw people into their pathology with their vivacity, enthusiasm and open flirtatiousness. The HPD person's predilection for drama compels conversational strategies that are self-focused. All the HPD person's efforts are directed toward becoming the center of attention at a party, or any other social gathering.

All discussion with a HPD person will concern only his or her personal interests. All conversation will be self-focused. Though highly magnetic in their body language and presentation, their emotional expression is extremely shallow. Their speech lacks detail and is notably superficial.

Narcissistic personality disorder:

People with NPD have an elevated sense of self-importance and a deep-seated need for admiration. Like the psychopath, the narcissist essentially lacks empathy for others. Though they might pretend to be swelling with confidence, while beneath all this pretense lies an extremely vulnerable and fragile person who is intolerant of criticism and suffers from well-hidden low self-esteem.

NPD is disruptive in many areas of life. Work, academics and most importantly, relationships suffer because of the NPD person's behavior. People with this disorder are generally unhappy or displeased with everyone and everything around them and often become angry if not given special treatment by others. A narcissist is not pleasant to be around.

Grandiosity is a defining feature of NPD. People with NPD believe themselves to be the most important person in the world and the epitome of the virtue, charm and human excellence. They are convinced that all they do is without reproach. This feature of NPD overlaps with the same tendency in APD (psychopathic) people.

Cluster C personality disorders:

Disorders in this cluster are characterized by timidity, accompanied by anxiety and fearful thinking or behavior. They are subdivided into three categories.

Avoidant personality disorder:

People with AvPD exhibit and experience feelings of inadequacy and extreme sensitivity and are always concerned about the opinions of others. They are easily intimidated by others and find themselves socially inadequate. These tendencies can result in avoidance in all spheres of life, like work, academics, and family responsibilities. Often, any form of social interaction is avoided. Avoidant behavior also adversely affects professional outcomes. AvPD people tend to miss deadlines or neglect to schedule meetings, which creates friction with colleagues in the workplace (when they are engaged in any kind of employment).

Shyness, together with an overwhelming sense of inadequacy and/or unworthiness characterizes this condition. Extremely sensitive to the possibility of rejection, AvPD sufferers pre-sabotage interpersonal relationships to prevent them from taking route (self-sabotage).

Dependent personality disorder:

People with DPD show extremes of neediness. Their demands and "clingy" behavior are overwhelming. In most cases, this clinging eventually develops into separation anxiety.

These patterns begin in early adulthood and manifest in many settings and contexts of life. DPD arises from a self-perception of inadequacy and the inability to manage the basic demands of life. This results in DPD people being completely dependent on others to fulfill their basic needs, as well as their emotional needs.

All criticism or disapproval is seen in a starkly negative light and usually results in self-sabotage and the loss of self-worth. People with this disorder deliberately seek relationships in which they are dominated in order to achieve a sense of protection (often over-protection).

DPD people find it very difficult to initiate independent action, as they are dependent on others for validation in the decision-making process. They avoid positions of responsibility and when faced with situations where an important decision needs to be made, feel extremely anxious and impaired.

Obsessive compulsive personality disorder:

OCD sufferers struggle with a perfectionist nature, are inflexible and have a compelling need for order and strict control over routines and circumstances. Such people readily become upset and angry in situations in which they believe they're thwarted from taking charge and being in control of things. They become extremely agitated if the external environment does not function according to their will and desires.

Anger is also not expressed directly but in an indirect way. A sort of moral indignation is often modeled, generally over petty issues that most people would ignore. A person with this disorder is inordinately particular about methodology and the order in which things are done to accomplish any given task. If the OCD person's methodology is not followed, it becomes difficult for him to function. Often, OCD sufferers find that maintaining personal relationships is problematic.

CHAPTER 4: DIAGNOSIS

The Diagnostic and Statistical Manual of Mental Disorders (DSM), published by the American Psychiatric Association provides details of the symptoms and clinical characteristics of all personality disorders. Mental health providers follow this manual for the purpose of arriving at diagnoses.

The criteria set by DSM must be met in order that patients may be accurately diagnosed with a particular personality disorder. Pinpointing the presence of a personality disorder can sometimes prove to be difficult, as symptom overlap in a variety of personality disorders is common within the three acknowledged clusters (see Chapter 3: types of personality disorders, above). Obtaining an accurate diagnosis requires time and effort, but ensures that the right treatment is prescribed.

Generally speaking, a person with a personality disorder will exhibit:

> ➢ Persistent long term and marked deviation from societal and cultural norms and expectations.

➢ Behavior that causes significant distress or leads to the impairment of personal, social and/or occupational situations.

Usually, personality disorders will have an adverse effect in at least two of the following areas of the person's life:

➢ The manner in which they think, perceive and interpret themselves and the people around them.

➢ Their emotional responses.

➢ Their behavior with family members and other members of the society.

➢ Their ability to control their impulses.

Most people with a personality disorder are capable of leading normal lives. They seek psychotherapeutic treatment when they reach the point at which they recognize they're unable to cope with a stressful situation or the social demands placed upon them. This is the best case scenario. In many cases, people with personality disorders are not diagnosed for many years and sometimes, for the duration of their lives.

The symptoms of many of the personality disorders listed above are entirely manageable. If you recognize three or more of the symptoms for any of these disorders in yourself, a friend, or loved one, it's advisable to consult a mental health professional for further advice. Such a professional, as well as any treatment plan arising should undertake all diagnoses.

CHAPTER 5: GETTING TO KNOW THE PSYCHOPATH

According to the fourth edition of The Diagnostic and Statistical Manual of Mental Disorders (DSM), published by the American Psychiatric Association, a person is recommended to undergo screening for diagnosis as a psychopath if he/she has:

> ➤ Exhibited sustained antisocial traits from the age of 15.

> ➤ Exhibited a pattern of utter disregard for the rights of others.

> ➤ Violated the rights of others.

Symptoms of a Psychopath

The most unfortunate fact about being entangled by the manipulation and ruthless behavior of psychopaths is that they live largely undetected among us. Most people today are somewhat acquainted with the psychological makeup of psychopathy and the damage it does to society. Psychopaths manipulate the people around them and heartlessly subject them to abuse, at work and at home.

We all know of people with psychopathic tendencies who heartlessly use and manipulate those around them. Many of us may have even been subjected to their abuse at work or in our homes. While it's not necessarily true that psychopaths are prone to crime, what they do to the people around them is a form of sophisticated psychological torture. Living with a psychopath is not unlike living in a personal hell for this reason'.

Blatant lies and false emotions are employed to manipulate targets. The psychopath does this with an absolute absence of compunction. They are incapable of feeling any. A psychopath is able to manipulate others with ease and without hesitation. Such behavior fulfills the psychopath's need to control and demean.

Studies show that psychopaths lack guilt, empathy or remorse. Their actions are completely devoid of even the basic understanding of these emotions. They consider their actions to be entirely justified and can't conceptualize that there is a pathology at work. The difference between right and wrong is an alien concept to the psychopath.

Human emotions like love, sensitivity, joy and sorrow are not within the ability of the psychopath to experience. Their life is that of a planet revolving on its own axis, entirely for its own sake. Psychopaths are consumed with their own importance. Their pathology is typified by an almost inconceivable egotism.

A person with at least three of the following symptoms may be a psychopath:

> ➤ Inability to conform to lawful social norms.

> ➤ Deceitfulness.

> ➤ Lack of foresight/ impulsivity.

> ➤ Extreme sensitivity.

> ➤ Aggression.

> ➤ Resorts to physical violence or assault.

> ➤ Recklessness or lack of concern about the safety of others.

> ➤ Total disregard for their own safety.

> ➤ Cavalier attitude about honoring financial obligations.

> ➤ Irresponsible behavior.

> ➤ Unable to retain employment due to inconsistent behavior patterns.

> ➤ No sense of remorse about having hurt or damaged others.

Symptoms of a pre-psychopathic child

Signs of psychopathic behavior can be detected in early childhood. The following signs should be noted:

> ➤ Escalating patterns of violent acts over a period of time.

- ➤ Constant bedwetting.

- ➤ Suicidal tendencies in an aggressive child.

- ➤ Desperate attempts to get attention.

- ➤ Disturbing thoughts and actions.

- ➤ Increased isolation.

- ➤ Prolonged mental illness resulting into destabilization of a child's mental development.

- ➤ Callous or unemotional behavior.

It's important to note here that diagnoses of psychopathy cannot be arrived at in the case of children. That said, pre-psychopathic traits are detectable in children and adolescents. There is currently a great deal of discussion around the idea that early detection may offer hope for containment, or even cure of the disorder. (Read more about pre-psychopathy in children in the chapter on the favorite haunts of psychopaths).

CHAPTER 6: WHO'S AFRAID OF THE BIG, BAD PSYCHOPATH?

Psychopaths can be entrepreneurs, politicians, CEOs and other successful individuals who have never committed any violent crime or spent time in a prison. They may have committed violations of a different sort.

Psychopaths exploit people, drain them physically, financially, mentally and emotionally and wreak havoc in their victims' lives. They may be disguised as businessmen or elected officials. In such powerful roles, psychopaths use their power for selfish ends. As employees, they are treacherous and undermining.

Medical experts estimate that about between 1-3% of men and just under 1% of women suffer from Anti-Social Personality Disorder. This means that 4.5 million men and 1.5 million women in the United States alone are psychopaths. Mental health professionals usually diagnose people with APD as psychopaths. The designation can, however, encompass people with Borderline Personality Disorder and Narcissistic Personality disorder, also, depending on manifestation of symptoms. The sex of patients is also a determining factor as women tend to be more frequently diagnosed with Borderline Personality Order than psychopathy, even in the event of symptomatic manifestation of APD.

In 1993, Dr. Robert D. Hare published the book '*Without Conscience*'. The main focus of his book was raising the general public's awareness about these predators who walk freely in our midst. It was also written with the intention of providing victims with hope. After an encounter with a psychopath, people's lives are shattered. They often find it very difficult to cope.

Dr. Hare believes the general public needs to be aware of the traits of a psychopath. Awareness can help people identify them when they cross our paths. Knowledge can allow us to protect ourselves from the trauma of encountering a psychopath by learning to deal with their behaviors, or to avoid involvement with them entirely.

Research has proven that 25% (one in four) of those convicted of a felony are psychopaths. The other 75% of felony inmates share many psychopathic traits. This is a fundamental reason for convict recidivism (repeat offence, resulting in re-incarceration).

Psychopaths may be criminals, but you will come across them in your daily life, too. According to Dr. Hare, a psychopath "touches virtually every one of us."

A word of caution

The manifestation of one or two psychopathic traits is not sufficient for a diagnosis of psychopath and only a qualified mental health practitioner can correctly diagnose someone as a psychopath. While it's tempting to believe that we can recognize psychopathy in others by reading about it, it's probably true that no one reading this is a clinical professional. It is with the professionals that we leave the work of diagnosis. A serious condition like psychopathy demands such trained attention.

The best way to deal with psychopaths is to avoid them completely. If this is not possible, seek the counsel of mental health workers or other medical professionals.

Dealing with psychopaths on your own may be extremely dangerous. There is a strong likelihood of their behavior becoming worse when they feel they've lost control of a situation, or have been identified as a psychopath. While it's possible to manage some situations, not all psychopaths, or situations involving a psychopath are manageable. Seek help.

CHAPTER 7: DRS. HARE AND CLEKLEY

Dr. Robert D. Hare, a criminal psychologist with in excess of four decades' experience as a researcher into psychopathy, is responsible for what is probably the most important diagnostic tool in this the field, the Hare Psychopathy Checklist. In the confusing and complex world of psychology, this checklist is used even in criminal courts to determine whether or not the offender in the docket is a psychopath.

Dr. Hare's website is named after his highly respected book, *Without Conscience*. Without Conscience, in both instances, provides a valuable resource for enhanced public understanding of psychopathy.

Only clinical professionals use Dr. Hare's Psychopathy Checklist, as the foremost diagnostic tool available. Various forms of the Checklist are used for different purposes. These include the Hare P-Scan, used as a method of detecting the possibility of psychopathy and as an indicator of potential criminal behavior. There is also a version of the Checklist specifically geared to youth diagnoses.

Dr. Hare's checklist identifies the following traits in psychopaths:

- Smooth talk and charming superficial manners – a pleasant, helpful façade erected to gain the trust of victims.

- Perception of being superior to others.

- Restlessness and hyperactivity. A constant need for entertainment, or compulsion to be engaged in some activity.

- Deception and lying.

- Emotional "absence" or flatness

- Violence.

- No sense of right or wrong or guilt and hence, no remorse.

- Shallow response to tragedy, trauma, injury to others (or animals). No feelings of grief.

- Lack of sympathy or empathy. No recognition of harm they cause to others.

- Sympathy-seeking. Instilling a sense of vulnerability by playing on the insecurities of others. Playing the victim in order to manipulate the emotions of others.

- Tendency to take advantage of the generosity of others.

➢ Lack of moral values.

➢ Promiscuous sexuality.

➢ Poor impulse control.

➢ Setting unrealistic goals based on their own grandiose perception of own achievements and talents.

➢ Refusal to acknowledge wrongdoing; flight from accountability.

➢ Irritability when plans and goals are interrupted.

➢ Unable to succeed in a marriage; may have several short-term marriages.

➢ Petty criminal behavior that can be traced to youth.

➢ Flexibility about breaking the law and bending rules.

➢ Revocation of conditional release (having probation revoked)

➢ Criminal versatility. (Psychopaths aren't specialists and delight in variety.)

The Hare Psychopathy Checklist is a well-researched, exhaustive document developed over time and subject to constant revision to reflect ongoing research. It is the most widely employed and reliable diagnostic tool currently in use for the purpose of diagnosing psychopathy.

While writing his PhD, the future Dr. Hare discovered the work of American Psychiatrist, Hervey M. Cleckley, through his important 1941 book about psychopathy, *The Mask of Sanity*. Dr. Cleckley's book and subsequent work became some of the most important to be done in the field of psychopathy in the twentieth century. Even today, Dr Cleckley (now deceased) is regarded as having made crucial contributions to the clinical community's understanding of the disorder.

Cleckley was also responsible for the now controversial diagnosis Multiple Personality Disorder. It was his case study that led to the production of the 1957 film, Three Faces of Eve. Today, Multiple Personality Disorder is known as Dissociative Personality Disorder and despite controversy arising, Dr. Cleckley is remembered as a pioneer in its study.

An evolutionary hint?

Cleckley's explorations into psychopathy are also somewhat controversial in that they contend it's a deviation from the human family, due to its affective deficit. He states, "The psychopath is simply an asocial or *anti-social* individual who has never achieved the developed nature of *homo domesticus*".

Dr. Cleckley identified the social nature of human beings as one of its defining characteristics and hinted that the psychopath's inclusion in that family was tenuous in the absence of this characteristic. It would be going too far to suggest Cleckley's intention was to assert that psychopaths were less than human, in terms of their evolutionary status. It's fair to say, however, that he was pointing to a mutated version of humanity realized in the emotionally devoid person of the psychopath.

If psychopaths are asocial or anti-social and sociability and communalism are ontological to humans, what does that mean? Are they an evolutionary blip? Are they a mutation?

Are they a version of humanity we don't yet understand? These questions continue to demand answers and Dr. Cleckley was the first to implicitly ask them. In that alone, his work is revolutionary.

Today, a debate exists in philosophical circles around a possible evolutionary link to psychopathy, suggesting that the psychopath is a sub-specie of humanity. The absence of emotional traits that distinguish humanity from other animals and genetic factors that contribute to the disorder have opened this discussion.

Anthropologists Henry Harpender and Patricia Draper have compared the social and asocial/anti-social traits in two disparate tribes to examine environment as a contributing factor. The question posed is whether this factor impacts the social nature of humanity on an evolutionary level (generationally adaptive).

Their 1998 study into the social organization of the Kung bushmen and the Mundurucu villagers found striking differences between the two, concurrent with the respective physical settings of the groups. The Kung Bushmen lived in the harsh and inhospitable setting of the Kalahari Desert, which required diligence and co-operation by all members of the community in the reproduction of daily life (including the sourcing of food). The Mundurucu lived in the Amazon Basin, an environment rich with food sources, requiring much less effort and co-operation on the part of the community.

The Kung, due to the challenges presented by their physical environment, formed strong family bonds and benefited from cohesion in the greater community formed by these staunch family units, resulting in what could be seen as a quintessentially human social order.

In contrast, the Mundurucu, in a less demanding physical environment, featured social stratification and even anti-social behavior. Males, disengaged from the reproduction of daily life, entertained themselves with gossip and seeking power in the community. Harpender and Draper also observed pandering by the males in the pursuit of obtaining sexual attention from females, as well as deception for that purpose.

Interestingly, harsh environments appear to promote social systems that demand the input of all members in concert and seem to be those which most readily promote societal health and "pro-social" behaviors. Conversely, excessive comfort would seem to be fertile ground for anti-social tendencies and exploitation.

Could idle hands really be the Devil's helper? Perhaps not, but the tribal comparison of the Harpender/Draper study merit further investigation. Could anti-social behaviors be nurtured in the midst of such abundance and the indolence they seem to provoke? Is that anti-social behavior a clue about psychopathy and where it came from?

Anthropologists Harpender and Draper's work is still being examined and Brent Kopenhauer Jr.'s discussion of their findings is provocative in its explorations. It features an examination of various evolutionary hypotheses following Cleckley's original statement concerning psychopaths and human ontology.

Others concerned with the study of psychopathy are looking at the possible evolutionary link to psychopathy. In their study Is psychopathy a disorder or an adaptation? Lianne J. Leedom and Linda Hartoonian Almas explore the possibility that psychopathy is linked to the practice of nepotism. They find in favor of psychopathy as a disorder, with nepotism being defined as a "pro-social activity" in its efforts to advance family members due to the familial association (contrary to its negative connotations for most of us).

Dr. Cleckley's seminal hint about psychopathy and evolution may yet find an explanatory link. For the timing being, though, the discussion is one of many in the philosophical and clinical communities seeking answers.

In Dr. Cleckley leading edge work, Robert Hare found his calling, embarking on a life of delving into psychopathy and building on the work of Dr. Cleckley to promote further understanding. His Hare Psychopathy checklist, now considered the disagnostic cornerstone for the disorder, is his brilliant legacy and a fitting continuation for the work of the iconic Dr. Cleckley.

CHAPTER 8: THE PSYCHOPATH'S WORLDVIEW

Psychopaths are emotionally vacant, with an inability to perceive the world as it truly is. Non-psychopaths perceive the world based on past experiences, understanding of them and on emotional responses to these. Psychopaths have no such benchmarks or scales to measure the reality of human experience in the world, so their perception of it is distorted.

The world of a psychopath is characterized by boundless and insatiable need, particularly a ravenous hunger for power and authority.

A psychopath's acquisitiveness is compulsive and all consuming. In their quest to draw to themselves as much of everything they desire as possible (believing they deserve it by virtue of their self-perceived innate superiority), psychopaths are willing to do whatever is required to get what they want. Extortion of material goods and money is achieved through the employment of bullying, threats and subterfuge, without the slightest compunction. In the mind of the psychopath, the end justifies the means.

Psychopaths entertain themselves by finding ways to exert psychological domination over others. Their manipulative skills are highly developed and their able to coerce and bamboozle those around them into doing whatever it is they want them to do, legendary. Their manipulation causes untold suffering to their targets/victims. Not only are psychopaths uniquely unperturbed by the suffering of others - they derive great pleasure from it.

Psychopaths are masters of spinning sad little tales to generate the sympathy of others. They know what sympathy and empathy are, even though they don't personally experience these emotional impulses and know precisely how to ignite them in others. Engendering the sympathy of others is a tool of manipulation and permits the psychopath to mimic the behavior of non-psychopaths by appearing to have a similar emotional life. In fact, they have no such life.

Lying is like breathing, to a psychopath. When confronted with their lies, they compensate and recover by inventing new lies to cover up the old ones. Psychopaths have little interest in the event their concocted stories contradict one another. They will deny this with shocking alacrity.

The memory of the psychopath is selective (or at least, psychopaths would have the rest of us believe it). They will tend to remember precise statements you made in the distant past and will not hesitate to use this information against you for the purpose of manipulation. At the same time, they will conveniently forget anything they said to you. A psychopath is never at fault. A psychopath can't be held accountable. A psychopath doesn't care whether you know the truth of the matter or not. The only truth is their truth.

Psychopaths firmly believe that all things (including people, who are objectified by psychopaths) are tools to be exploited to the fullest extent for their sole benefit. People exist for them to use as objects of their machinations. How many people they hurt, ridicule or cause distress to is not their concern. They are shallow-minded and empty people who treat others callously.

While psychopaths may model a fondness of animals as part of their complex mimicry of non-psychopathic behavior, they are not equipped to treat them with anything but contempt. They're not really interested in doing so either, as animals have an even lower status in the psychopath's world than human beings do. Criminal psychopaths are known to "practice" sadism on animals in their youth.

Psychopaths are adept at projecting the image of being revolutionary thinkers or supporters of the poor or down trodden. They give the impression they are noble, humble and magnanimous. In reality, they are extremely self-centered and could care less whether people starve or have access to clean water. Pretending to care is part of the psychopath's carefully constructed veneer of normality, which exists only for the sake of convincing others that he is just like them.

Arrogance is a defining hallmark of the psychopath. The grandiosity of their self-image is of an enormity most of us find difficult to imagine. Their egotistical character allows them to see themselves as characters in an epic novel (their lives) or film; the protagonists of their cinemascopic and endlessly fascinating saga. This grandiosity leads them to believe that everything they do is not only justified, but also necessary and that anyone who dares challenge them is fundamentally disordered. Psychopaths have no difficulty projecting their own traits onto others, because they are completely unaware that these traits are their own. While being innately self-aware in terms of their egos and self-importance, they present a lack of self-awareness that almost amounts to unconsciousness.

Psychopaths work hard to impress those around them with "big fish stories" of their almost impossible, praise-worthy achievements. While it's often patently obvious they're lying, they're unstoppable once they've commanded the attention of anyone who will listen. The terrible thing is that so few of the psychopath's listeners are willing to call a stop to it.

In sum, psychopaths are superficial charmers with an incredible communicative facility. They have an almost preternatural ability to make others feel special by saying all the right things. It's in these traits of charm and the art of telling people exactly what they want to hear the psychopath's ability to deceive and dissemble lies.

You don't see them coming. When they finally strike, you are broadsided; in shock. The person you believed to be so charming and engaging turns out to be monstrous beyond anything you might have imagined.

Psychopaths can't change. They feel no need to and in fact, see themselves as not only blameless, but also perfect and entitled. Others are seen as flawed and of interest only insofar as they might serve a purpose for the psychopath in helping to meet his all-consuming need to power, domination and acquisition of material goods.

CHAPTER 9: A STUDY IN MANIPULATION

The Arch Manipulator

As stated earlier, we tend to think of psychopaths as monstrous serial killers or rapists, creeping around in back alleys at night, stalking the next victim. Thirsty for blood and fiending for a fresh victim, our popular image of the psychopath is only realistic in some instances.

The psychopath can be pretty well anyone such as a doctor or dentist, your neighbor, a friend, a lover or your child.

Psychopaths wear tailored suits, or stilettoes, uniforms or overalls. They're in the boardroom, or on Main Street, or seated in the front row of your history class. They're speaking from the podium and pulpit...selling you insurance.

Psychopaths are found in all areas of life and not all psychopaths are the bloodthirsty serial killers of our popular imagination. Most of them blend right in with the rest of us.

In essence, they *are* us. They're mutated incarnations of humanity in its most cruelly inhumane, emotionless form. The psychopath might even be sleeping next to you tonight, in your marital bed.

In her book about the trial of Adolph Eichmann (tellingly subtitled "The banality of evil") Hannah Arendt wrote the following:

"The trouble with Eichmann was precisely that so many were like him, and that the many were neither perverted nor sadistic, that they were, and still are, terribly and terrifyingly normal."

It's in that terrible "normalcy"; an ability to slither into the world of the sane with such facility as to go undetected (even in the highest political or corporate office), that the true horror of the psychopath lays.

A psychopath's appearance and behavior in the world is difficult to distinguish, at the outset, from that of anyone else.

Over time, though, how do we come to know that the person we're dealing with is a psychopath? What are the red flags that cause the scales to fall from our eyes; the mask to fall from the psychopath's face?

One of the most telltale hallmarks of the psychopath is the ability to manipulate just about anyone to arrive at a desired outcome. There are numerous methodologies people with this condition are capable of employing. One thing is certain, though – the psychopath is an arch manipulator.

How do they do it? First off, psychopaths need a certain type of target. Targets are chosen for perceived malleability, as well as a lack of confidence and sophistication. Psychopaths look for the weakest link in any chain and then pull on it until it breaks.

As stated in the Introduction, psychopaths have a systematic pattern of behavior. This behavior routinely plays out in three parts, described below.

Identifying targets - Assessment:

Psychopaths are endowed with a unique and powerful ability to pick targets out of a crowd. They have a type of radar for those vulnerable to their machinations; those who will not know they're being played until they're so deeply involved in the psychopath's games they can't get out.

Certain people most readily fit the psychopath's profile for an ideal target. They share distinct personality traits prized by this predatorial manipulator.

The Psychopathy Self-Report Scale assesses the level of psychopathy in those completing and self-identifying traits from a select inventory. It's been discovered that the higher on this scale a psychopath scores (in terms of traits self-reported), the more skillful the psychopath is in identifying targets.

Body language is a prime indicator of likely targets for psychopaths. Factors suggesting a lack of confidence in the potential target are especially attractive.

The study Psychopathy and Victim Selection: The Use of Gait as a Cue to Vulnerability, identifies the way potential targets walk as one means psychopaths select for vulnerability. One of the cues psychopaths look for in this area is an asynchronous (not synchronized; uneven) gait.

Shorter steps and slower walking speed also serve to identify potential targets.

Other non-verbal clues, like eye contact, posture and gestures figure prominently in the mental inventory a psychopath takes when making a vulnerability assessment. A failure to make steady eye contact indicates a submissive nature in the potential target. Small, inhibited gestures indicate a lack of confidence, expressed in a lack of commitment to the gesture.

While clearly a target is never responsible for the behavior of a psychopath, or victimization of any kind, it's clear that certain non-verbal cues attract the attention of people with this psychological profile. It's also probable that targets displaying non-verbal traits attractive to the psychopath have developed these over time as the result of previous ill treatment of some kind. This information, contained in gait, gestures, posture and other non-verbal cues, informs the psychopath that the potential target is vulnerable. The study cited above determined this to be the case and that a sample of incarcerated psychopaths chose targets with a history of ill treatment most frequently.

Once the psychopath has picked out a target displaying body language similar to that described above, he gets closer to determine whether the target is naïve, lacking in worldly experience or shy. These are traits that seal the deal for the predator psychopath, as they indicate a person with the sort of temperament he seeks – passive, accepting and sweet natured to a fault. The targets most vulnerable to the psychopath's manipulative charm are the easiest prey because they wear their insecurities and history of abuse on their sleeves.

Another personality trait prized by the psychopath in a target is empathy (the ability to "feel with" another). People with high levels of empathy present a delightful challenge to the manipulative psychopath. Identifying the tendency of a target to be caring and empathic is an invitation for the psychopath to incite these feelings. A psychopath relishes the opportunity to use the target's empathy against her, weaving hard luck stories that would make a stone weep. The target is drawn in via empathic response to this story and the psychopath knows it.

To determine a potential target's empathy level, psychopaths will spend some time in the initial phases of what amounts to a "seduction" (regardless of the relationship's nature) teasing out this information. Pushing all the right buttons to determine if the target is empathic enough to fall hook, line and sinker for the psychopath's elaborately woven tales is a specialty of this predatorial, arch manipulator.

"My wife just left me."

"I recently had to put my dog down."

"I just lost my job."

All these are "trial balloons" sent up by the psychopath to elicit a response from the target. Does the target cry? Perhaps relate a parallel tale from her life? Does the target say they're sorry for the psychopath's loss and take a sip of coffee, holding his gaze? All responses to these trial balloons are analyzed for the level of empathy expressed, indicating the target's vulnerability. These are tabulated and added to non-verbal cues to arrive at an assessment.

If the target is lucky, the psychopath will write her off and keep moving (as sharks must in order not to die). If the target is not so lucky, she's about to get the ride of her life at the hands of a predator who has marked her for manipulation.

Manipulation – taking ownership

The psychopath is a manipulator *par excellence*. In fact, artful manipulation is what psychopaths are best at.

As detailed in the section above on assessment, the psychopath's ability to read people by observing their mannerisms and speech patterns. Systematic in their detailed assessment of potential targets, psychopaths begin their manipulation of these unfortunate victims the moment they open their mouths, during the first conversation.

Even before that moment, psychopaths ensure they present a pleasing, attractive appearance, taking great care to charm in precisely the manner in which they know they will elicit a positive response from the target. Their affability, though, is a carefully constructed façade. Almost hypnotic in its effectiveness, the psychopath's veneer is smooth and seamless. Coupled with an ability to put targets at ease, this first line of a psychopath's attack.

As the relationship with the target intensifies, the psychopath employs flattery in order to subdue any residual tendency on her part to resist, or question his motives. Gaining the trust of the target is key to the success of this phase of the relationship. If trust is not established, the psychopath will walk away empty-handed. He will not be successful in obtaining the money, power, sex or influence he is seeking from whatever relationship he's been engaged in.

The façade or mask of the psychopath is expressly in place to fool targets. The ability of psychopaths to lie without compunction and artfully so, can disarm even the most intelligent and discerning person.

Psychopaths play their targets with a predatorial expertise that is almost undetectable, but certain verbal clues can give them away. Jeffrey Hancock, communications professor at Cornell University has studied psychopathic speech patterns. Working with colleagues at the University of British Columbia, he's concluded that verbal irony and deception are the two defining characteristics of these, but has also studied the actual use of words and themes in psychopathic speech to identify clues that can tip people off to the fact they're conversing with a psychopath. The paper, Hungry Like the Wolf: a word pattern analysis in the language of psychopaths, which appeared in the journal Legal and Criminological Psychology in 2012, was jointly written by Hancock and UBC clinicians, Michael T. Woodworth and Stephen Porter.

Hancock et al note in their research, that words indicating causal themes like "so" and "because" are indicative of psychopathic speech. Without the capacity to feel guilt, psychopaths are only too ready to justify themselves by providing a thoroughgoing rationale for their actions.

He left you standing by the side of the road *because* he had to be somewhere else.

He embezzled funds from the company *so* they could afford a vacation he felt he deserved.

Psychopaths also tend to talk more about material needs in the course of a conversation (food, sex, money) than they do other human needs. In the absence of an emotional life, that is the psychopath's focus. Psychopathic speech was also found to be punctuated by more verbal disfluencies (uh...um..er, for example) than that of non-psychopaths. These interruptions in the course of spoken statements, for psychopaths, are opportunities to organize their thoughts into a convincing, plausible format, in order to better manipulate their targets.

The work of Jeffrey Hancock and his colleagues provides a valuable window in the linguistic world of psychopaths, but their manipulation techniques are complex and highly polished.

Once a psychopath has convinced his target that she is all that an a side of fries, employing every trick from overwrought, effusive praise to the presentation of gifts to demonstrate his undying adoration, more sophisticated means of manipulating the target come into play. With trust established, the manipulation machine that is the mind of a psychopath kicks into high gear. At this point in the game, some of the psychopath's most treasured instruments of torture (and that's what it is) come out of the toolbox and are applied with clinical precision and relentless dedication.

Intermittence – praise interrupted

Just as the target begins to feel at ease with the psychopath, floating around on a cushiony cloud of the compliments the psychopath has been priming the pump with; things slowly begin to shift.

At first the change in the treatment the target receives from the psychopath is almost imperceptible. The target senses something's wrong. The psychopath's mood is suddenly unpredictable and sullen. No longer the bearer of gifts, or the crooner of sweet words of undying admiration, the psychopath has become not only less effusive with the praise, but has begun complaining about the target's shortcomings.

Perhaps the Blues are being sung (in the kind of plaintive wail only a psychopath can muster).

"You don't really love me."

"I've given you everything, but you don't appreciate me."

"This is exactly what happened with my marriage/last relationship/mother/boss."

Nothing the target does serves to calm or placate the woeful psychopath and the litany of ills soon grows in volume and duration.

"You're so hurtful. Everybody says so."

"You only think of yourself."

"You're so greedy!"

The target reels with confusion, trying to figure out what possibly could have precipitates this change. From being the center of the known universe, the target has now been reduced to a source of indignation and irritation by the psychopath, who works over time to convince the target that he is the aggrieved party. His largesse rebuffed by a lack of appreciation and recognition, the psychopath sulks, withdrawing the attention he once so freely gave the target.

Psychopaths know exactly how to get the attention of their targets, because they've not only spent time in incisive assessment of their character, they have continued building on that knowledge to find their targets' weak points and triggers.

But just when the target has reached the end of the rope, the psychopath returns to his "normal" self, again offering the positive reinforcement he has withdrawn. The relief felt by the target at this turn of events is indescribable. The original euphoria returns. What the target is unaware of is that the psychopath is establishing a pattern, to be repeated whenever necessary in order to keep the target off balance and vulnerable.

Typically, psychopaths employ this technique as a means of softening the target up for future demands (planned well in advance). The target will learn, over time, that non-compliance with the psychopath results in the withdrawal of affection.

Inhibition – disallowing negative emotions

As the target is pulled deeper and deeper into the psychopath's dark world, it will become increasingly clear that this relationship is a toxic rollercoaster. The target begins to challenge the psychopath and if there's one thing a psychopath doesn't tolerate well, it's any challenge to his egotistical control and domination.

Any attempt by the target to discuss a perceived problem is met with intransigence on the part of the psychopath. Not only will he not give an inch, instead of focusing on the concerns of the target, he will turn his attention to the nature of the target's emotions, deeming them unacceptable and invalidating them. Resolutely refusing to discuss these concerns, the psychopath turns the tables by re-focusing the discussion on the inconvenient and unwelcome emotions being displayed by the target.

This behavior only exacerbates the target's desolation with the situation, adding frustration to an already confused and embattled state. The inhibition of emotional responses on the part of the target are an important strategy for the psychopath. It takes the heat off him and places it on the target, even though the target is not at fault. It allows the psychopath to maintain a position of presumed moral superiority. It provides the psychopath with one more way to dominate the target by ensuring there is no balance or predictability. Balance and predictability are undesirable in the psychopath's world. They provide a solid footing for the target from which to resist the downward spiral this toxic relationship is now in the midst of.

Passive aggression – abuse disguised

Name-calling is a form of abuse which is extreme, but which can be disguised in various ways.

A psychopath can call the target every name in the book and then claim this was done as a way of somehow instructing the target in his or her shortcomings. Words like "weakling", "bitch", "idiot", "pathetic" or "needy" may be deployed to deliberately hurt the target, but veiled in the language of concern for the target's wellbeing.

"If you weren't such a weakling, you might actually get that promotion."

"You might have more friends if you weren't such a bitch."

"You are pathetic when you say things like that"

"Your neediness is off putting."

By framing the insults in play as constructive and not destructive, the psychopath again shifts the blame to the target. By framing abusive language as reflective of shortcomings in the target in need of remedial action, the psychopath has gotten away with saying things that should by no means be tolerated by anyone in the context of a healthy relationship (of any nature).

Triangulation – the threat of replacement

As though the target didn't have enough to deal with, the psychopath will often employ another form of passive aggression – triangulation. This method either hints at or openly declares the presence of another, competing party to the relationship.

The psychopathic ego is boundless and energetic. It pleases psychopaths to believe that they're in demand and sought after. Whatever these many admirers seek from the psychopath, be it sex, entertainment, or professional association, psychopaths revel in knowing (and letting it be known to targets) that they are on every speed dial list in town.

The practice of psychopathic triangulation is another technique by which psychopaths keep their targets in a vulnerable state of insecurity and doubt. By broadly hinting that the target isn't the only game in town and that, in fact, the psychopath is playing at multiple tables, the target is forced into the position of obsessing about the psychopath's other interests.

Where is he tonight?

Did he take lunch with that other guy in accounts?

Is he considering turning somebody else's unpublished novel into a screenplay?

The psychopath's need for the belligerent and bullying domination of the target aims to create a situation that demeans and debilitates. The target becomes increasingly unable to mount a defense against the incessant gamesmanship of the psychopath. Up is no longer down. Day is now night.

The specter of competition is deliberately raised, because the target is so "lucky" to even know the psychopath; to even be a blip on his hyper-attuned radar. Here is the primary motivation for the psychopath's triangulation – instilling in the target the belief that he is a "hot property" the target should be eternally grateful to be in the appreciable orbit of.

What triangulation amounts to, in practice, is an implicit threat. The psychopath, by engaging in this strategy, is telling the target that he is able to end their association at any time. From one moment to the next, he might decide to jettison the relationship and disappear forever, "ghosting" into the ethers precipitously and finally. Triangulation serves to keep targets in a state of fear that they could be abandoned at any time.

Gas lighting – historical revisionism

The psychopath is a creature spun of mendacious malice. This cannot be denied. One of the most heinous of the psychopath's techniques of manipulation and one of the most baldly deceitful and malicious is gas lighting.

Gas lighting is the practice of denying words and events that have, in truth, been said or have actually transpired, with the full knowledge that the denial is an enormous and deliberate lie.

The lie, of course, is not told for its own sake. Rather, the lie is told for the sake of (once again), destabilizing the emotional equilibrium of the target.

Imagine someone you know denying, bald-faced, to have said or done something you know very well they did. Imagine the inscrutability of a psychopath, staring back at you (looking you straight in the eye) and lying with no hint of compunction.

"I never said that."

"I never did that."

"That never happened."

Despite the fact the incident is as a fresh as a newly plucked daisy in the target's mind; that the memory is indelible, the psychopath will persist in maintaining that he is telling the truth. With steadfast and frigid self-righteousness, the psychopath will insist that his version of events is the only version.

In the target's attempt to provoke an important discussion, unwitting permission has been granted the psychopath to employ another implement of torture. By simply reminding the psychopath of an incident or discussion that incites the discomfort of the psychopath, the target has opened the gates of hell.

Gas lighting, if persistently and diligently practiced, will eventually result in the total collapse of the target's ability to discern the truth and even reality. The target will come to question her memory and sanity and again, the psychopath will succeed in pushing the target off balance.

Recognizing the strategies of a psychopath is a helpful skill for everyone to have. If you're unfortunate enough to have a psychopath in your life, knowing the strategies employed will provide you with the knowledge you need to derail them.

The most important skill those dealing with a psychopath can have is the ability to discern that one of the foregoing strategies is in play. Once you've determined that this is the case, the next skill required is the ability to rise above it. While this isn't easy, it's necessary. You are not a helpless victim. You're a human being with the right to live in peace, free of the gaming of psychopaths. Nobody deserves to be intellectually and spiritually attacked by a loved one, colleague, friend, or family member.

It's in your power to change the game by following these general guidelines:

- ➤ Don't react. Maintain a neutral facial expression.

- ➤ Listen carefully and then say you appreciate the psychopath's point of view, but don't share it. Don't elaborate it, even if the psychopath insists.

- ➤ Remove yourself from the discussion. This will leave the psychopath talking to the wall.

- ➤ Talk to a clinical professional.

If you are entangled with a psychopath, it's important that you seek professional counsel. Attempting to do more than defuse toxic communications without the assistance of a mental health expert will only make matters worse. If you have absolutely no recourse but to continue whatever relationship it is you're having with the psychopath, don't try to do it alone. Seek help.

If you can, leave. You can't help this person. Psychopaths don't change and there's absolutely nothing you can do about it. Walk away and take your self-respect and sanity with you.

CHAPTER 10: FAVOURITE HAUNTS OF THE PSYCHOPATH

Psychopaths can appear in any walk of life, or sector, but they gravitate toward certain scenarios. These appeal to his need for domination, power and grandiosity.

Romantic and sexual relationships are a particular favorite of psychopaths. These provide the opportunity to hold another human being completely in his thrall. Through the employment of pandering, sexuality and feigned emotional intimacy, psychopaths take particular pleasure in not only breaking hearts, but also psyches.

Where work is concerned (psychopaths need to eat, too), there are some key areas that provide lush fields for the machinations of the psychopath.

In his book <u>The Wisdom of Psychopaths: what saints, spies and killers can teach us about success</u>, research psychologist Kevin Dutton identifies the ten professions found most attractive by psychopaths, as follows:

CEO

Lawyer

Media (TV/Radio)

Salesperson

Surgeon

Journalist

Police officer

Clergyperson

Chef

Civil servant

This list may surprise some. Some of the professions included aren't normally those associated with psychopathic traits, but the author as those most dominated by psychopaths identifies these.

Does anyone else find it troubling that surgeons and police offers are listed here?

Dutton contends that the regulation of emotions is a key indicator for success in any field. This factor is of greater importance in certain professions (those listed above, for example). Suppose your surgeon was prone to emotional outbursts in the midst of your hip replacement procedure, for example?

Perhaps a psychopath with a scalpel isn't such a horrible prospect after all. Perhaps the SWAT team psychopath, engaged in a firefight with terror suspects, is the calm in the eye of the storm.

The ability to bear up in stressful situations when others crack may be a redeeming feature of psychopathy, rendering those with the disorder uniquely suited to high-pressure work. Is this a silver lining? According to Kevin Dutton, that may be the case.

There may be significant value inherent in people with the disorder, if their traits can be employed to the good. The prospect is a hopeful one in a world that hosts as many as 70,000,000 psychopaths.

Perhaps the ability to diagnose and channel psychopaths into fields in which their unique personality traits serve a purpose is the wave of the future. For the time being, the truth is that psychopaths leave a trail of destruction where ever they go.

Let's take a walk though some of the psychopath's favorite haunts and look at how psychopathy plays out in them.

Spinning the web – the psychopath in love:

Psychopathic gamesmanship in the realm of romantic relationships is well known. How many people in this world have been caught in the web of these spiders of emotional manipulation? How many have regretted every laying eye on the psychopath who rocked and then ruined their world?

Once a psychopath has identified and reeled in likely a target, he proceeds to work his particular magic. The flattery drips like honey from his mouth, as he covers the target in effusive praise and adoration. This is easy for a psychopath, as the communication skills associated with this condition are considerable. They are masters of ornamental, insincere, florid speech and possess the ability to make those they target feel they've embarked on a magic carpet ride of unparalleled wonder.

As the relationship progresses and the psychopath's professions of undying love escalate, the target finds herself in the midst of a "whirlwind romance", being swept off her feet by this psycho in shining (albeit faux) armor. He can't get enough of her. He texts her every 10 minutes. He tells her she is the most incredible woman he's ever known and that he's never known anyone even remotely like her. Her hair, her eyes, her lips – they're all cosmic in their perfection.

This "love-bombing" (the practice of bombarding the target with extravagant praise and adoration) continues unabated, ensuring that the physical realization of this apparently epic love affair arrives as quickly as possible. Sex, in the world of the psychopath, is the silver bullet to total domination of the target. The target's lack of sophistication; her naiveté, are desired by the psychopath for precisely this reason. If she's easy to convince, she's easy to dominate. Chances are the woman chosen is either a virgin, emerging from a long-term relationship or marriage (which may have been with a similarly abusive person), or grievously inexperienced in the ways of the world in confrontation of sexual affairs.

The psychopath's ability to put a woman who fits this profile precisely where he wants her is almost supernatural. Once he gets her there, he ensures she remains where he wants her to be there for as long as he desires.

He demands sex constantly.

And he's good at it.

Soon, the target is lost in the psychopath's vortex of pandering and sex, caught inextricably in this spider's, sticky, intricately spun web. Eyes deep in hearts and flowers (not to mention the pervasive "sex haze" the psychopath has created), the target can barely discern what day it is, much less how bad things are about to get.

For psychopaths, though, sexuality is not the profound human experience it is for most of us. For them, it's a means to an end and that end is unchallenged power over the target. Recognizing the vulnerability of the target to his charms, the psychopath uses sex for the sake of controlling her in order to obtain the complete control and domination that is, in truth, his biggest "turn on".

There is nothing a psychopath loves more than playing a part – stepping into a role and playing it to the hilt. They do this to achieve their ends (whatever these are in any given situation) and sex is no exception to this rule. While discussion of sexual "performance" is reasonably popular in mainstream society, in the world of a psychopath, the word takes on its most literal connotation. It's all an act for the benefit of convincing the target that the psychopath is somehow invested in the relationship; that he can't get through his day without having sex as with her as many times as possible. The target is overwhelmed by this lusty satyr's attentions, hardly believing the intensity of the sexual connection she has with him.

She shouldn't believe it. Psychopaths have the acting abilities of Michael Fassbender when it comes to sex, because its only value in their world (unlike that of their hapless targets) is as a currency to obtain what they ultimately desire – the truest aphrodisiac of psychopathy – power. Whether that power is wielded for the sake of money, or to obtain other consideration valuable to the psychopath, the truth is that power and domination and the primacy of the psychopathic ego is the only love people with this disorder can ever know. It may even be the end in itself.

For the psychopath, power is not only the greatest aphrodisiac. It's the only aphrodisiac.

Snakes and ladders – psychopaths in suits

Dr. Robert Hare once famously said that he was not "...studying psychopaths in prisons, I'd do it at the stock exchange". He wasn't kidding when he said that and it's not just a problem on Wall Street. Psychopaths and the corporate world have a symbiotic relationship.

Just as they do in romantic relationships, psychopaths in business settings will single out targets according to similar criteria, but for different reasons. Who can be used as a stepping-stone to where he wants to get in the organization? Who can be exploited to land in that corner office, with the gold-plated pension plan, the company car and the limitless expense account? How can the unfortunate obstacle (someone who sees through the psychopath, or someone with a job the psychopath wants) be dispatched? The brass ring the psychopath has set his sights on is on the other side of this human roadblock.

An unassuming chartered accountant toiling in the corporation's bowels, unrecognized for his hard work? A middle manager, embittered by fruitless years of attempts to ascend to the executive offices? Perhaps that underpaid, insecure administrative assistant with total access to corporate files and every secret there is to know; secrets the psychopath might deploy for the sake of advancement?

Which of them will the ambitious, power-hungry psychopath adhere himself to in order to achieve his ends?

In their book, *Snakes in Suits: When Psychopaths go to Work*, by Dr. Paul Babiuk (an industrial-organizational psychologist) and Robert D. Hare (progenitor of the original psychopathic traits inventory, discussed earlier in this book), explore the prevalence of psychopaths in the corporate and business world. Incredibly, psychopaths find a home in this arena with ease and this book provides an examination of those who manage it, through case studies and analysis.

In the corporate world, psychopathic traits like extreme egotism and grandiosity serve people with this condition well. Traits like these are not only tolerated, but prized in corporations and can lead those who model them straight to the CEO's office. The charisma of the psychopath, slithered into a suit in the guise of normal person, is ideally suited for the high-powered business world, in which profit is king and the power to achieve it dominates all. Corporations are a target rich playing field for the manipulative psychopath and a favored arena for his pathological gaming. As Kevin Dutton has discovered in his work as a research psychologist, the role of Chief Executive Officer is the psychopath's most prized vocation.

Psychopaths have an enviable ability to manage the impressions others have of them. Through the employment of superlative communication skills and the absence of some of the social inhibitions other people struggle with, the psychopath's pathology is read in a corporate setting as the sort of enthusiasm and bravado that sets a leader apart.

Once in a position from which to pull the strings, having manipulated himself there with glacial calm, what more is there to do? It's at this point the psychopath may well flee from the chaotic moonscape he's made of his little corner of the corporate world, leaving damaged careers and reputations behind. As he bolts for the door of the executive suite, stock options stuffed in his pockets, the lights come on and everyone involves gasps in horror. Perhaps, though, he is dragged away by the FBI.

Perhaps the psychopath has created a massive Ponzi scheme (pyramid investment), or created a system of toxic mortgages which bring the economy of the entire world close to collapse (as happened in 2008). Maybe the psychopath has abused his expense account, or the corporate jet, or engaged in an elaborate scheme to evade corporate taxation. Whatever legacy the retreating psychopath leaves in his ruinous wake, it's bound to have a lasting impact and the Annual General Meeting promises to be an unmitigated bloodbath.

Winner of 26 international awards, the film *The Corporation* examines the nature and character of the societal institution known as the corporate *entity*. Based on the book *The Corporation: the Pathological Pursuit of Profit and Power,* this film explores issues arising from the corporation's status as an "entity" (a being). If the corporation is a "being", then what sort of character does it have?

According to filmmaker, Joel Bakan and his collaborators, that character is pathological and further - psychopathic. If Bakan is right and the corporation is, in fact, a pathological institution with all the traits of psychopathy, then is it any wonder psychopaths find in it such a welcoming home? Corporate will to power, compelled by the profit motive, and very closely resembles the agenda of a psychopath. The domination of all for the sake of ultimate power and an unquenchable demand for primacy (ego) point to a bizarre manifestation of psychopathic pathology in institutional form.

The idea that psychopathy might somehow benefit society by serving corporate institutions, due to that sector's adaptability to psychopathic traits, is certainly attractive. Perhaps in the future, researchers can find ways to control the baser instincts of the pathology in order for it to function to society's benefit in the realm of corporate governance, instead of to its detriment.

Candidate psycho – the psychopath in politics

The world of 21st Century politics is fertile ground for the nurturing of the garden variety psychopath. Not unlike the corporate world, the political sphere is primarily concerned with power. In a world of unlimited donations to political candidates via PACs (political action committees) and SuperPACs (PACs on steroids), it's also a great place to prosper financially. Psychopaths love nothing more than unlimited power and financial gain, so politics could not be a more perfect stage onto which a greedy, egomaniacal psychopath might make an entrance.

Maybe the psychopath is a political wonk with aspirations to make it to the highest office in the land. An elected official, a Chief of Staff to someone installed in high office, or even the holder of that high office could be a psychopath. It's almost nightmarish to believe that people with this pathology could be in a position to determine the future of entire nations, or even the world. The problem is, it's not only possible, but also probable.

Imagine, if you will, a world governed by psychopaths.

The calculating mind of a psychopath, so adept at reading people and tabulating traits that indicate ready targets for their manipulations, is the mind of a successful politician. That is not to say that all politicians are psychopaths. This would be like saying that all butchers are Sweeney Todd (fictitious London barber of the Victorian era, famous for murdering his clients and baking their remains into meat pies).

It's true, though, that a political mind is a calculating mind. It weighs situations to arrive at strategic formulas. It analyzes polling data to determine where the greatest support is in a campaign run – who to call; where to "pull" the vote to get it to the polls on Election Day. It sizes up not only the competition, but also supporters and advisers, discerning by observation the personality profile of those who will remain loyal. It flags potential enemies to either eliminate or keep near. Following the advice of legendary Chinese military strategist, Sun Tzu, politicians know well to keep their friends nearer and their enemies nearer. In short, the calculating mind of the psychopath features traits imminently desirable in a politician.

A veneer of easy charm and charismatic appeal also serve the psychopath in politics. Political candidates are, in these latter days, chosen quite expressly for the ability to come across as everybody's best friend; somebody Joe or Jane Public might choose to enjoy a beer, or a cup of coffee with.

This ease in public settings is part of the psychopath's pathological make up, due to a low response to stressors involving high profile, public settings; stressors that terrify other people. Psychopaths thrive on such contexts and view them with relish. The idea of holding an audience in the palm of one's hand is nothing short of euphorically transcendent, in the mind of a psychopath. In such a proposition resides the possibility of commanding the attention of perhaps thousands or even millions of people, simultaneously.

What could be a more delicious proposition for a psychopath?

Just as all politicians are not psychopaths, all psychopaths are *not* politicians. The grandiosity of a psychopath may not always line up with his intellectual capacity. Some psychopaths, while giving the impression of possessing an extraordinary intellect, are of average intelligence, but superior skills of manipulation and "mimicry" (an ability to ape the behaviors of those they seek to resemble).

"Candidate Psycho" boasts a particular combination of psychopathic traits uniquely suited to the political sphere. As outlined above, charisma, verbal facility, an analytical approach to sizing up people and strategic acumen are traits sought after in politicians. A psychopath modeling all these traits in a physically appealing package is Candidate Psycho.

The Netflix series House of Cards is the story of one such political animal – Frank Underwood. This fictitious character is the exemplar of Candidate Psycho. From the moment we meet in the first season, Frank is busy plotting his way to the Oval Office from his position as Chief Whip in Congress for his political party.

Underwood's genius is undeniable. His ability to play Congress people off one another to attain his ends, employing all manner of subterfuge and intrigue, is grounded in his intimate understanding of the traits of all those he manipulates. He knows their weaknesses, is aware of old grudges they hold, fodder from personal lives that might be used to provoke a scandal (and thus ruin a political career). He moves Congress people around like chess pieces, destroying one career as he builds another up, ever evaluating each move made for its utility in moving him closer to the highest office in the land.

In one scene, Underwood employs the basest form of bullying to neutralize a challenge from a union leader, provoking his challenger to the point the unfortunate target hauls off and punches him in the face. This is a marvelous illustration of the ability of a psychopath to trigger people in a very deliberate manner, provoking a response that the target and not the psychopath must wear and shoulder the blame for. Underwood walks out of the encounter unscathed, with the exception of a cut lip. Willing to take one in the kisser to nullify a challenge to his unmitigated power indicates that Underwood is a psychopath of monolithic proportions.

What truly gifted psychopath wouldn't do the same?

Underwood's manipulations indicate pathology at the very outside edge of the psychopathy scale, as they don't stop at the destruction of careers, but extend to the destruction of human lives. An out-of-control Congressman is unblinkingly dispatched in an elaborately faked suicide. A journalist with information that could ruin Underwood were it to leak into the public domain, pushed in front of a train. Not once does Frank Underwood flinch, because he believes with every fiber of his being that all he does is justified.

As a classical psychopath, Underwood sees himself as the protagonist in the vast sweep of his life; an underdog who will do whatever is necessary (even murder) to achieve the highest office in the land and keep it for as long as possible. He justifies himself by believing he's destined for the office and even that he's its rightful owner. Surely, no one else on the planet could have what it takes to sit in the Oval Office; in that big leather chair, pulling the strings and pushing the buttons. The Frank Underwood character in House of Cards is a brilliant study of psychopathic grandiosity, manipulation and the superficial charm employed by psychopaths to attain political power.

In House of Cards, Frank Underwood keeps his eyes on the prize until he attains it, ascending to the office of the President of the United States of America. A master of the game; an arch manipulator, Frank Underwood bears all the traits of the psychopath *par excellence.* Even though this is a fictitious character, House of Cards begs the question – how many of our political leaders are psychopaths?

How many Frank Underwoods lurk in the halls of power, fingers itching to be poised over the big, red button; a final act of cold-blooded disdain for an unworthy world?

One of you – a psychopath in the House of God

Not unlike corporate and political structures, religious institutions (as opposed to what are popularly known as cults) provide a legitimizing structure in which psychopaths can embed themselves. The respectability of a recognized denomination in a mainstream Faith system is a like a petri dish for a psychopath (mad scientist of manipulation). The possibilities offered by this context are highly appealing to psychopaths.

The pulpit itself is a powerful draw. From this position of control (not dissimilar to the political podium), the psychopath is invested with an authority not otherwise available. Before him, rapt with attention, is the flock ingesting whatever it is he feels like doling out on any given Sunday.

Religious institutions – intended to be places of reflection, healing and peace, are too often targets for this worst of all possible elements. Places of worship provide promising predation grounds for psychopaths and where better to profit fully from these target rich centers than the pulpit?

It's easy to look to famous cult leaders as the exemplars of psychopaths in religious or quasi-religious settings, but these are only the tip of the iceberg. What's beneath the surface is a much more sinister reality and one which has touched the lives of too many trusting, faithful people. Under the cloak of respectability provided by such communities, the psychopath can quietly manipulate his way to the power and wealth he lusts after.

In the context of the Roman Catholic Church alone, the global pedophile scandal can be pointed to as the work of probable psychopaths. The fact that many of the perpetrators and enablers were able to continue operating within Church structures bears witness to a principle feature of psychopathy: intimidation and bullying. It's speculated by former insiders like Fr. Robert Hoatson (now de-frocked and an advocate for victims of the scandal) that those guilty were shuffled from parish to parish and diocese to diocese because of their threats. Bishops, archbishops and even cardinals were threatened with exposure for various ecclesiastical infractions, according to Fr. Hoatson, enabling perpetrators of crimes against children and families to continue operating with impunity. Even Bernard Cardinal Law, who presided over the scandal in the diocese of Boston, was airlifted to safety in the third most powerful see of the RCC, Santa Maria Maggiore in Rome.

Law's must be the softest landed ever enjoyed following a transatlantic flight in the history of aviation.

Contrary to popular belief, the RCC is not the only denomination of the church to suffer from these abuses. It is only the most notorious. The probable reason for that notoriety and the fact that these abuses were permitted to flourish is the institution's secrecy. Psychopaths are deeply attracted to institutions with this characteristic, because it allows them to perform their manipulations without having to fear the accountability of public scrutiny.

Secrecy is the psychopath's best friend.

Another great ally of the psychopath in organized religions is their hierarchical and authoritarian nature. Particularly at risk are denominations and other religious structures that adhere to strict interpretations of the Bible and what constitutes belief. A catechism or confessional statement (statement of belief) is a launching ground for the psychopath to shut down all accountability for wrongdoing.

Tools like blasphemy (insulting or showing contempt for God or institutions associated with God), demonic influence and clerical authority are ripe for employment by a psychopath. In a community that takes such things seriously, these stand ready to justify the psychopath's machinations and serve them.

Religious institutions, together with other "affinity groups" (intentional communities in which certain beliefs and principles are held in common by all members), like political and social organizations, provide the psychopath with a structure for his gaming. According to Drs. Robert D. Hare and Paul Babiuk, authors of *Snakes in Suits,* such groups are often the setting for what they term "affinity fraud". To commit such fraud, a psychopath insinuates himself into the group and exploits the beliefs and principles he allegedly holds in common with other members. Such fraud might take the form of embezzlement, for example.

Dr. Hare likens a psychopath engaged in such activities to a "fox in the henhouse". The fox comes into the henhouse and takes a good, long look around. It then identifies targets to use as stepping stones to the position it wants to slyly ascend to. As the fox makes it way towards its objective, it manipulates and bullies. It does so by exploiting the institution's foundational beliefs. As with the example of the psychopath in love (who uses the target's love as a weapon), the psychopath in the House of God uses the beliefs of the community against it, mercilessly exploiting them as cover.

Adherents in any given religious institution tend to share a belief in the inherent goodness of humanity. A belief in seeing the best in others, particularly those who are members of the group (members who ostensibly share the same beliefs), is a communal myopia the psychopath is only too willing to use to his advantage. The credulity of all around the psychopath serves only to enable his machinations, making it possible to defraud the institution, leaving it completely blindsided.

Before anyone knows what's happening, the treasury of the mosque, synagogue or church has been looted and the psychopath in question is long gone. In the event that one set of clear eyes has been trained on this fox in the henhouse, perhaps the owner of those eyes blows the whistle before things get to that point. But if they do?

Chances are the psychopath will again exploit the foundational beliefs of the group, saying the accuser is "possessed by the devil", or is a "blasphemer". Then again, the psychopath could go the "heartfelt contrition" route and throw himself on the mercy of the congregation, expressing sorrow for his misdeeds and begging God's forgiveness. In doing so, the psychopathy turns the nature of the community against it, using it to avoid accountability for his misdeeds.

Once everyone's convinced the fox is endlessly sorry for having mangled all the hens leaving a pile of feathers in his wake, he will scamper for the exit, the last of the wretched birds in its jaws.

The devastation of the fox's adventures will be witnessed for years to come, as the faith community attacked seeks reconciliation between its members; friendships of a lifetime ravaged by it.

"There will be no new roof, or parking lot extension this year", the congregation is tearfully advised.

Because it wasn't just the hens the fox made off with.

It was the building fund, too.

Chucky in the house – childhood symptoms of psychopathy

The 1988 movie, Child's Play, tells the story of a doll inhabited by the malevolent spirit of a serial killer. The doll walks, talks and entertains homicidal rages. Based on the true story of a doll said to have been similarly possessed, the supernaturally animated doll in the film, "Chucky", has terrified audiences all around the world.

But what if your apparently normal child were to suddenly manifest the symptoms of psychopathy?

What if Chucky was in your house?

It's known that psychopathy can appear in children as young as five. This doesn't suggest that professionals can arrive at a reliable diagnosis for people of this age. The Diagnostic and Statistical Manual (DSM) V, actually precludes such a diagnosis, due to the fact that young children cannot be said to have exhibited a sustained symptomatic pattern, due to their tender age.

Regardless, child candidates for a diagnosis of psychopathy display behaviors similar to those of adult psychopaths, including high levels of manipulation, a callous disregard for the disposition of those around them and affective flatness (lack of emotion).

A researcher at Florida International University, Dan Waschbusch, has been studying children who display callous-unemotional traits. Children who display these traits are now understood to be at risk for an adult diagnosis of psychopathy and are considered, clinically speaking to be "pre-psychopathic". There is, however, a great deal of disagreement on the subject.

In May 2012, the New York Times published the controversial story of Michael, 9-year-old son of Anne and Miguel. Written by Jennifer Kahn, the article was provocatively entitled "Can you call a 9 year old a psychopath?" Kahn's article has given rise to a maelstrom of discussion on the topic of pre-psychopathy in young children. Read it here:

Michael's mother, Anne, relates that at the age of three, the child's behavior underwent a pronounced shift. This occurred following the birth of a second child. Wild tantrums would persist for hours at a time, at the slightest provocation. Until age 8, the situation continued, accompanied by episodes of violent acting out, including the destruction of clothing with scissors and punching holes in walls,

At their wits end, Anne and Miguel took Michael to a therapist, but the resulting diagnosis ("first born syndrome") did little to improve the situation. Anne noted a strange ability on the part of her son to "flip" between uncontrollable rages and a calm, seemingly rational and almost adult demeanor. These shifts would be almost instantaneous, leaving mom's mind reeling. Michael was also prone to manipulative behavior and an apparent disinterest in the effect it had on those he trained it on.

Finally, after years of competing diagnoses that led nowhere and mounting frustration at failing to find an answer to their questions about Michael's behavior, the family's psychologist referred them to Dan Waschbusch (see above).

Waschbusch assigned an assistant to conduct interviews with Michael's parents and the education professionals he was engaged with at school. When the data was tabulated, it was discovered that his ranking on the Inventory of Callous-Unemotional (CU) Traits was nearly two standard deviations outside "normal" range for these traits. This placed him at the severe end of the spectrum.

Michael eventually attended a course of treatment for CU children with Dr. Waschbusch, but Anne remains unsure that this improved the situation. She fears Michael may just have learned to manipulate others with greater sophistication.

Increasingly, clinicians are finding that childhood traits indicating callousness, a lack of emotion, or a lack of empathy, point to the possibility of psychopathy. "Fledgling psychopaths" are set apart from other children with behavioral problems not only by these traits, but also by violent episodes, impulsivity and hostility.

Paul Frick, a psychologist at the University of New Orleans has studied children with pre-psychopathic traits for two decades. Frick is on the leading edge of research in the field of children who exhibit CU traits and with his colleagues in the mental health field, has developed methodologies which convincingly demonstrate that these children are at risk for adult psychopathy.

It's known that the amygdala (see section on genetics and brain function) plays a significant role in the mind of a psychopath. Damage to this portion of the brain may account, at least somewhat, for the lack of empathy modeled by people with the disorder. This effect has also been observed in pre-psychopathic children. It has also been established that genes are a contributing factor to psychopathy and that this is especially true in male children.
.

Nobody wants to call a child a psychopath. Essentially, labeling children with such a designation at the dawn of their lives seems almost cruel. However, the possibility that pre-psychopathic or "fledgling psychopaths" can be identified and treated is being explored. Such a possibility would have enormous implications for society.

If it's possible to not only identify, but treat early onset symptoms of psychopathy, the hope that psychopaths might be treated before growing to adulthood (and thus, full blown psychopathy) is well worth exploring.

What if the early signs of the disorder could be treated? Could this mean that psychopathy might eventually be eliminated entirely?

Neuroscientist Kent Kiehl places the cost of psychopathy to society at $460 billion per year. In terms of judicial and penal infrastructure, fraud and victim impacts, the real cost to society is enormous. Add to this the damage done to so many by psychopaths in all areas of life; all professions. It's clear the cost of this disorder to society at large is tremendous.

So while it may seem cruel to pigeonhole children with a diagnosis of psychopathy, separating diagnostics from determined outcomes is an important key to the possible discovery of a means of either controlling or eliminating psychopathy as a societal problem.

The University of Vermont's study, published earlier this year in the Journal of Abnormal Psychology suggests that if pre-psychopathic traits are detected early enough in a subject's life, there may be hope for treatment. This study examined a sampling of 150 11-17 year olds (both male and female) in a juvenile detention center. All subjects examined in the study had been identified as displaying CU traits.

Tim Stickle, a psychology professor at the University discovered that most of the subjects did not fit the profile of a psychopath, regardless of the fact they displayed CU traits (believed to be foundational to the disorder in children and adolescents). He found that these subjects indeed felt emotions like fear and had developed coping mechanisms to mask their emotions. The effect was to cause them to appear to be modeling CU traits to researchers on Stickle's team. In fact, these subjects were coping with emotional trauma and disguising the emotional fall out as a method of self-preservation.

The study concluded that CU traits in children and adolescents could, at least in some cases, be treated. It found, for example, that cognitive behavioral therapy (CBT seeks to change patterns of thinking toward changing resulting behavioral patterns) holds out hope for these young people. The findings of Stickles' study were based on a more rigorous testing methodology than is normally used to identify pre-psychopathic traits in children and adolescents. Stickle believes that using a similar diagnostic could serve to narrow the field among children displaying callousness and affective flatness, toward more accurately identifying truly pre-psychopathic subjects.

Among truly pre-psychopathic subjects, there may be hope in terms of early detection and intervention in order to manage symptoms before they "harden" in adulthood. With that possibility in mind, though, it's instructive to re-visit the example of Michael, the 9 year old identified as pre-psychotic.

Michael's time in CU treatment seems to have yielded no change in his behavior. As a probable pre-psychopathic subject it seems that Michael, at the age of 9, is either already impervious to all efforts to modify his psychopathic tendencies, or that the right treatment for someone like him has not yet been found.

What is known about psychopathy, though, is that it has quasi-genetic origins. The possibility that damage to certain sections of the brain may exacerbate the effects of genetic factors, points to a solution beyond the modification of behavior (see section on genetics and the brain). As clinical research continually improves our understanding of psychopathy, uncovering new secrets of the human brain and its functions each day, it's possible that the Michaels of this world may one day have access to relief of their symptoms.

Also known is this – there is no known treatment or cure for adult psychopathy. It is a disorder that has, until this day, eluded treatment. The greatest hope for the containment and eventual elimination of the disorder and its deleterious societal effects lies in ongoing research. Pre-psychopathy in children and adolescents, as well as a greater understanding of genetics and the brain (and the part they play in the making of a psychopathy), continue to hold out hope.

Until then, they walk among us.

Regardless of the setting, the psychopath's *modus operandi* varies little. Whether the psychopath (or the psychopath's target) is male or female, an institution, a lover, a corporation or an entire government, the psychopath will use all the same moves; the same strategies, to attain primacy and domination.

Psychopaths will always employ a general patent of assessment-manipulation-abandonment, easily recognizable by those who are informed about the disorder. It's important to recognize common strategies employed by psychopaths to avoid becoming a target and ultimately, a victim.

CHPATER 11: FACING OFF WITH A PSYCHOPATH

Are you a target? Are you observing psychopathic traits in a lover, friend, colleague or family member? Your local Congressional representative? Your rabbi? Following are some common target/psychopath scenarios and how you might respond to them.

Do the twist – dealing with the lies

Situation: Your psychopath is intelligent and will play on your emotions to weasel their way out of any and every situation. Confronting a psychopath is not fun, because such confrontations cause great discomfort for people with this disorder. Instead of discussing situations with you, a psychopath will twist your words, gas lighting you into submission. As discussed in the section on Manipulation, psychopaths use this technique to skew your sense of equilibrium, causing you to question your memory of event and your sanity.

Sometimes, in response to your attempts to discuss a problem, psychopaths will seek to incite your sympathy as a method of avoidance. For example, you question psychopath about late night binge drinking, telling them you're worried about it becoming a habit. The psychopath may launch an epic rationale for the behavior saga, claiming to be depressed and saying he didn't want to trouble you with it all. By doing this, the psychopath hopes to make you feel guilty about raising the subject in the first place.

Woe is the psychopath – and you're just a big meanie.

Response: Trust yourself. Listen to the psychopath's tale patiently and then re-iterate your concerns. End the conversation, regardless of whether the psychopath believes it has concluded or not. The message is that you're onto the game and you're not playing.

Sure I'll help do that (no I won't)

Situation: Some work around the house needs to be done. Psychopaths rarely volunteer to do anything at all that won't directly benefit them and your psychopath is no exception. In fact, you have to ask every time and rather sweetly, at that.

The psychopath will not refuse outright (that would be way too honest). Instead, he will mount a façade of genuinely caring about the task at hand and having desire to help. It won't end there, though. Because you've had the temerity to ask the psychopathy to do something he doesn't want to do, he will make you feel as though they've been asked to move a mountain. This is a huge favor you're asking and a tremendous sacrifice of time and effort is being demanded of the psychopath to accomplish it. There will follow a great deal of huffing and puffing as the psychopath dithers, procrastinates and generally avoids actually doing what you've asked of him. The dramatic silence, punctuated with heavy sighs and perhaps the ganging of various household objects on tables (etc.), is the psychopath's way of saying "I don't want to".

Response: Know in advance that your request is going win you a command performance of the most cloying Greek Tragedy ever to be performed. Instead of going on the preferred trajectory of your psychopath, save yourself some valuable time. Elicit a clear "yes" or "no" answer from him. Regardless of what follows, keep moving. The chore will be done, at some point, but at least you've spared yourself the dramatic episode (and some time).

I didn't say that/do that

Situation: Psychopaths are known for making promises they can't keep. At the time they make them, they sound good. Your psychopath may promise something that's important to you, just for the sake of saying it and giving you the impression they give a damn. You remember the promise made very clearly. Where and when it was made and perhaps the contents of the promise, verbatim (word for word). When you remind the psychopath about this promise, he may pretend either to not remember having made it, or flatly deny having made it. Regardless of your repeated efforts to prod the psychopath's memory, he will deny his own words, or claim amnesia. This again, is gas lighting, a convenient out for psychopaths everywhere who make vain promises and a weapon they enjoy turning against the memory and sanity of their targets.

Response: Document. Document. Document. Keep a diary of all the psychopath's statements, recording the "whats" and "whens", as well as the words used. (An Excel spreadsheet may be equal to the task, in consideration of the volume of lies you may have to deal with.) This will have the effect of throwing the psychopath off kilter. It will probably also tick them off mightily. Your motives will no doubt be question. Employ one of the psychopath's own tactics and tell that you're becoming absent-minded and have taken to making notes in order to remember important conversations. Be sure to smile when you show your psychopath the detailed notes you've made.

The guilt train – to nowhere

Situation: Psychopaths are experts at organizing guilt trips. Their emotional manipulations can instill guilt in even the most resilient target concerning the most trivial matters. Psychopaths feel it's entirely appropriate to criticize you for every detail of your person. Talking, not talking, doing, not doing, the way you part your hair, the way you walk, your eyebrows - all are deemed ripe for picking at by psychopaths. The effect is that you wonder how you can fix your speech, you behavior, your damnable eyebrows to please the nitpicking psychopath.

Psychopaths will also buy you a ticket on the guilt train for unwittingly failing to satisfy an unspecified need of theirs. Their vagueness is deliberate. They don't want you know what the matter is, because that would preclude your taking a ride on the guilt train. You may not know what it is they need (as they haven't articulated it to you), but you *should* know (according to him) and you should feel really badly for not having had the good taste to satisfy it. The most ridiculous part is that when you actually try to meet a psychopath's expectations or take a stand about their passive-aggressive demands, he will turn the tables. The psychopath will, in the most irritable and unreasonable fashion, let you know that your participation was never required because he's perfectly capable of doing it all on his own.

Response: Refrain from justifying your perceived slight (because you didn't do anything wrong). Let your psychopath stew in his own toxic brew of passive-aggression. Don't engage in this battle over nothing and above all, don't set foot on that guilt train to nowhere. Tell your psychopath that you know he'll work out whatever it is that's bugging him; that he'll find a way to placate himself without your help. He's done it before. He can do it again.

Backtalk – sowing the seeds of confusion

Situation: Emotional manipulators never confront things openly. They prefer to talk behind other people's backs in order to shore up the possibility that they might be seen for what and who they are. They prefer to build false impressions about their targets in the minds of others. This pre-emptive strike methodology has the effect of immunizing the psychopath from scrutiny and thus, revelation that he is a psychopath. Putting the focus on the target as the guilty party builds sympathy in the community in which the psychopath operates (work, family, church, social circle).

Instead of coming directly to you with their demands and expectations, a psychopath will employ others tell you on their behalf. Friends, colleagues and family members will come to you expressing concern about your behavior toward the psychopath. They'll want to know why you did this or that to the poor, beleaguered creature. You will stare at them blankly, not knowing what on earth they're talking about. With knowledge of your psychopath, though, you'll know exactly where it came from. This game is one of the psychopath's favorites. Attempts to not only communicate with you in a roundabout way, but to plant negative information about you in the minds of others is a useful prophylactic against being unmasked. You look like the bad guy. The psychopath comes up smelling like a rose.

You want to go somewhere on a trip with your children, friends, or perhaps attend a convention. Your psychopath smiles pacifically at the news, claiming not to mind one bit if you go. Sure, he'll take care of the kids/workload/cat! He is happy for you and agrees that you deserve it.

So off you go, never knowing that in your absence, the psychopath has put abroad that you're a selfish, uncaring ne'er do well who has left him to shoulder your responsibilities. What a lousy thing to do! You return to the disapproving scowls of all concerned and the realization that your psychopath has been busy while you were away and not just with the kids/workload/cat.

Response: Find somebody who isn't a psychopath to look after the kids/workload/cat while you're away. In the event that you haven't reached this "zen master" level of psychopath management and have left the psychopath in charge, deal with the fallout of his stories directly. Tell friends, family members and colleagues your side of the story and ask that they not to repeat the psychopath's complaints. This will put the genie back in the bottle. Experience is your teacher. Next time, find somebody who isn't a psychopath (you know the rest).

Your problems pale in comparison to the psychopath's

Situation: You've had a crumby day at work. As try to vent about the events of the day, your psychopath goes off on a tangent about all the stress he's been under and how trying it all is. Almost as soon as you start venting, the psychopath will grab the microphone and start yammering into it about himself and his problems. Should you have the bad taste to interrupt, reminding the psychopath that you were talking and that he interrupted you, prepare for the onslaught of recriminations that will ensue as a result. Selfish, self-centered, egomania monster that you are, the psychopath will, without hesitation, project all his traits onto you. His face will be a study in pathos, as he expresses how deeply you've wounded him by not putting your own troubles on pause in order to quietly hear his litany of ills. The guilt train has once again pulled into the station and all because you were silly enough to believe that your psychopath might be even remotely interested in hearing about your day. Silly you.

Response: Look at the psychopath and with a straight face, say the words "Poor you." Walk away. Let the psychopath tell his tale of woe to the wall, even if your refusal to entertain it has caused it to become an angry rant worthy of a toddler. Let the psychopath howl. Sit in the kitchen until it dies down, perhaps sipping on a nice glass of Syrah.

Even if you find yourself trapped in an association, family, or other relationship (whether romantic or platonic) with a psychopath, all is not lost. Even if it's not possible for you to leave at this time, you have the power to shift the balance into something more closely resembling equity.

The psychopath wants to win – every time. The thought of not winning; of not obtaining what he desires is the psychopath's Kryptonite. By employing coping strategies that serve to disarm the power of the psychopath's manipulations, you can not only survive, but ascend to the "zen master" level of psychopath management.

Remember that the support of mental health professionals is always advisable. Running yourself into the ground as you attempt to manage your psychopath alone is not an option. Don't hesitate to ask for help the moment you need it.

CHAPTER 12: CASE STUDIES

We've examined the symptoms, behaviors, traits and favorite hang outs and outlined some strategic tools for dealing with psychopathic behavior. Now it's time to meet some real life psychopaths.

This sampling of case studies is in no way intended to be definitive. It is hoped, however, that it's broadly representative and instructive.

#1 – Criminal Fraud – financial abuse of seniors

The subject is serving time in federal prison for the felony of fraud.

During the course of #1's fraud career, lived out over a three year period, #1 employed deception and subterfuge, as well as high-level verbal skills and charm in order to defraud hundreds of senior citizens throughout the United States of their life savings.

Choosing his targets due to their vulnerability and tendency to trust, #1 relieved these people of everything they'd worked for their entire lives. His targets, as a result, suffered severe symptoms of stress that, in some cases, threatened their lives.

#1 has been referred to counseling, a process he has absolutely no interest in pursuing, although he feigns genuine interest in an effort to charm the counselor.

When the counselor advises #1 that three of his targets have died of heart attacks due to the stress he caused them, he suppresses a laugh. He proceeds to justify his actions and blame his targets, due to that fact that they were all adults and invested with the will to resist his appeals. He then turns on the counselor, accusing him of partiality in the conduct of his duties.

As a psychopath, #1 does not recognize his wrongdoings. He refuses to be held accountable, preferring to blame his crimes on the victims themselves for not having resisted. In classical psychopathic style, #1 laughs at the suffering he has caused, and then turns on the person who dares to mention it by impugning his character.

The nature of number one's crimes, the character of the targets (vulnerable senior citizens) and the methodology he employed to carry them out indicate numerous psychopathic traits.

#2 – Professional deception – the sexual abuse of children

#2 was a respected family doctor, much loved in the community. #2 was also a researcher at the local teaching hospital.

Over the years of his practice, rumors circulated about his contact with child patients. These were whispered around town until a local schoolteacher finally decided to blow the whistle and take her suspicions to the state medical board. Under investigation, #2 relinquished his license to practice medicine and retired.

Several years later, #2 died prematurely. His death opened the floodgates and one after the other, people in the community came forward with stories of #2's abuse. He had deceived the parents of numerous children into believing that he was conducting medical research that required her perform certain actions on the bodies of children. Manufacturing parental consent by way of deception, #2 convinced the parents of numerous children to surrender them to him to be abused.

None of the parents of the children #2 abused ever suspected that anything was amiss. He was a beloved family physician and child sexual abuse was the further things from their minds.

Over many years, number two convinced parents, the medical community at the hospital where he served as a researcher and the community at large, that he was just a kindly doctor. Through the employment of manipulation, the use of his respected position and community prestige, #2 was able to abuse children for year with the full co-operation of their parents.

The fact that #2 could engage in these behaviors while insisting that these children were being seen for research purposes indicates a brilliant and active mind at work. The deception and secrecy involved are the classical tools of psychopaths and especially those who seek impunity to sexually abuse children. #2's exploitation of the status associated with the medical profession is especially chilling.

#3 Between two diagnoses – BPD and psychopathy

#3's story is marked by behaviors generally associated with Borderline Personality Disorder, beginning in high school. Prone to outbursts, manipulation of those around her and lying, #3 displayed all the symptoms of BPL.

A schoolyard bully, #3 formed a clique and became a fearsome presence in her school. Known for her unpleasant demeanor, she regularly drew people into her small circle, and then jettisoned them when they became intransigent in the face of her abuse and bullying.

#3's employment history and relationships were marred by her serially anti-social actions. She was frequently fired for insubordination, or quit due to her own intolerance of having to work in the presence of those she deemed to be less intelligent.

Eventually, #3 had a child and lived with the father. Although engaged in a relationship with another man without the child's father's knowledge, #3, upon finding the father to be similarly engaged, kicked him out.

Her parenting skills proved to be deeply deficient, with the child considered by her to be a burden. A frequent habit of #3's was to leave the child with friends of relatives "for a few hours", only to return the next day. When questioned, she few into uncontrollable (sometimes physically violent) rages.

Her tendency to view others with contempt, coupled with her ability to draw others into her abusive vortex, indicate a personality on the cusp of psychopathy. What prevents such a diagnosis is not only #3's sex, but the tendency of women to exhibit behaviors more closely associated with Anti-social Personality Disorder's Cluster C neighbor, BPL.

It's often the case with women (as discussed earlier in this book) that a diagnosis of BPL is more routinely arrived at, despite the fact subjects often model many of the classic traits of psychopathy.

The conclusion of her clinician, in #3's case, is that if she were a male patient, she would be diagnosed as suffering from psychopathy. Due to her sex, though, a diagnosis of Borderline Personality was arrived at.

In fact, most patients receiving a diagnosis of psychopathy are male and most receiving a diagnosis of BPD are women.

The case of #3 begs the question – how many women psychopaths receive inappropriate diagnoses, due to their sex?

CHAPTER 13: SHAKING OFF A PSYCHOPATH

Strangely, people find it extremely tough to let go of toxic, abusive relationships. Even though they've been through an earthly hell and their lives lay in ruins around them, they can't seem to pick themselves up, open the door and walk out. Many will find this inertia in the victims of abuse difficult to understand, sometimes blaming the victims, themselves. But there are explanations for the inability or unwillingness of abuse victims to remove themselves from abusive situations. They question their own mental health and are often so emotionally wrung out, they no longer have the will to act.

The emotional makeup of the psychopath's target (for which they're expressly targeted), targets turn the blame on themselves instead of their tormenter. They believe they have invited the abuse, or perhaps deserve it, having internalized the gas lighting and other manipulative behaviors they've been subjected to. They stay, hoping things will change.   They promise themselves they'll do better, or that their abuser, himself, will suddenly change.

People in these toxic relationships hold on for several reasons:

> In a romantic relationship, the victim is still in love with the psychopath and unwilling to let go.

> There's unwillingness on the part of targets to let go of their original concept of the psychopath and to see him for what he is. Often, victims are the ones who discover the truth, as they tend not to listen to the commentary of others who've witnessed the psychopath's behavior. The shock of realizing their partner is a psychopath is too overwhelming for them to cope with.

> Victims tend to be vulnerable people who don't bear up well under the kind of stress psychopaths can create in their lives. They feel there's no way out, as they see no alternative to the situation they're in. Often, victims have no support system, having been isolated from sources of possible support by the psychopath.

> Many targets are plagued by the fear the psychopath will stalk them. This fear is not unfounded. Psychopaths, once exposed, reel with resentment at what the target has done. The cat's out of the bag and suddenly, the psychopath can be seen for what and who he is. Mortally wounded, he becomes obsessed with punishing his former target. Stalking the target is a form of intimidation that provides the psychopath with a taste of the power he once had over his former target, who's finally broken free.   Stalking may be

pursued online, in the physical world, or both. For the manipulative psychopath, stalking is emotional terrorism and represents a return to the normal dynamics of the relationship – a win.

> The victim has witnessed and experienced the white hot heat of the psychopath's rage in the past, or may even have been threatened with physical violence.

> The abuser is a family member, boss, or religious leader.

> The victim is part of a religious community that will shun or excommunicate those who aren't willing to put up with abuse from husbands and other male family members.

There are multiple and serious reasons some targets/victims can't remove themselves from the abusive relationship with a psychopath. In the last situation noted, there is not even a support system or clinical help to draw on in many instances. The community, holding values in common will join in condemnation of any deviation from those communal values. The community and its leaders may also have philosophical objections to any resort to mental health professions, or even counseling which isn't governed by that community's particular values.

It's important to keep in mind that even your best efforts can't change or cure a psychopath. There is no cure. They can't change. If you find yourself trapped in a relationship with a psychopathic abuser, all you can do is order your responses to the psychopath's actions in such a way as to defuse their destructive power and protect yourself and those around you.

See the Resources section at the end of this book. These may prove helpful. Please remember, though, that there is no substitute for professional help, which is strongly advised.

CHAPTER 14: CULPABILITY AND THE PSYCHOPATH

If, in fact, psychopathy is a disorder that originates in body chemistry, brain function and genetics, then are psychopaths, by virtue of these immutable factors, guilty for what they do?

How should psychopaths be treated once they've already committed a major crime? Should they be treated less severely due to their illness? Who should be blamed for their actions? Should their destructive (even murderous) behavior be blamed on their genes or their intentions? Should they be sentenced longer than other criminals as they pose a greater threat to society?

In recent years, psychopathy has become a topic of great interest in the area of moral philosophy. The last decade has seen many serious discussions and discourses on whether psychopaths can be held morally responsible for their harmful actions. The presence of psychopaths among us raises a host of ethical and moral questions.

While it's undeniable that psychopaths are challenged by circumstances well beyond their control, how far do these circumstances toward holding them harmless? Without no moral compass and the absence of normative human emotions, how does culpability apply to them?

While none of these questions can be definitely answered in this book, an examination of some of the research streams in this area of the study of psychopathy is of value. Philosophers, neurologists and anthropologists have all contributed to these findings and their input is both grounds for serious reflection in the question of culpability.

Do psychopaths know the difference between right and wrong?

Philosopher Neil Levy, in his paper Psychopaths and blame: the argument from content argues that in the absence of a moral framework due to the emotive handicaps represented by psychopathy, there is no basis for holding them responsible for their actions.

Those who don't know right from wrong can't be called upon to govern their actions according to the distinction between the two. Further, the psychopath's objectification of human life precludes the possibility of assigning any value to it. To a psychopath, people are means to an end; tools to be used to achieve his purposes. Levy argues that in the absence of intent, ideation of the intrinsic value of human life and the ability to discern what constitutes moral conduct, the psychopathy may not be blamed.

But in his summary of arguments from these perspectives, Jeff Danaheer argues to the contrary. In this summary, entitled *Can psychopaths be blamed for their actions? A summary of the empirical a philosophical arguments* Danaheer points out that psychopaths can, indeed, conceptualize moral imperatives. The problem, in his view, is not that psychopaths are unable to intellectually grasp moral concepts, but that they don't believe they apply to them, personally.

Danaheer also states that the claim psychopaths are unable to engage in Mental Time Travel (MTT, the ability to objectively view one's past and future and derive meaning from them, encompassing the consequences of one's actions) is not empirically supported and therefore not a fitting basis for Levy's arguments against culpability.

So the jury remains out, as philosophers tussle over these and other issues concerning the responsibility of those who have this disorder.

It's clear that psychopaths don't take responsibility for their actions. While they will freely admit to their actions, they fail to attach judgment values to them. Instead, the psychopath will seek to explain these actions through complex rationalizations. As pointed out by Danaheer, this doesn't mean psychopaths don't grasp the concept in play. It simply means they don't believe it applies to them. They believe it's for other people.

There are many questions around this issue and a decided divergence on the part of those addressing it via philosophical enquiry. On one hand, we say that psychopaths are unaware of the consequences of their actions and on the other, we know they painstakingly plan and calculate their actions, including their crimes, with forethought and calculated precision. Without displaying any emotion, they plot and execute their actions. Psychopaths show no regard or concern for the suffering of their victims. This is the key. While psychopaths are fully aware of what they're doing. They do not possess the emotional intelligence to understand why they shouldn't do it to begin with. That is not to say they're not responsible for those actions under the law.

If minor children can be tried as adults and subsequently jailed for their crimes according to the same sentencing structures (a debate well beyond the scope of this slim volume), then why shouldn't psychopaths be?

If the developmentally disabled can be executed for their crimes in US states that continue in this practice, then why can't psychopaths be?

Finally, the dysfunction in the brain of the psychopath (discussed earlier in this book) and the possibility that sections of it may be damaged should inform the discussion. The debate about culpability and psychopaths is about much more than moral philosophy. It's about chemistry and brain function. Surely these factors are not the fault of the psychopath.

Oxytocin, the moral molecule?

Paul J. Zak of the Aspen Institute, in his July 10, 2015 article in Time Magazine, discusses his work isolating the molecule, oxytocin. His book, The Moral Molecule: The Source of Love and Prosperity, is described on its Amazon page as a "revolution in the science of good and evil".

Dr. Zak's hypothesis develops the seed originally sown by Hervey Cleckley and his suggestion of an evolutionary basis for psychopathy. Zak argues that the oxytocin molecule is the source of the distinctly human, pro-social emotions – love, kindness to others and most importantly, for the purpose of this book – empathy.

The molecule is present in childbirth and breast-feeding and is produced by 95% of human subjects tested. Of the remaining 5%, about half Zak's subjects were in a less than sunny mood.

Of the other half, most met the diagnostic criteria for psychopathy.

Oxytocin has been called the "moral molecule" due to its role in governing pro-social, pleasant, communally motivated behaviors. Not unlike pheromones, the molecule is unconsciously detectable by human beings as a scent borne on those around us.

There are two primary factors capable of inhibiting oxytocin production. One is stress. The other? Testosterone (the male hormone).

Oxytocin, while present in all of us, can be inhibited by certain factors. Two of these are listed above. Another is physical or emotional abuse. Oxytocin receptors in abused humans or animals were found by Zak's research to be fewer in number.

Because oxytocin is part of the complex biochemical system that governs feelings of wellbeing and goodwill, it logically follows that the inhibition of its production can result in less noble impulses, including entitlement, selfishness and egotistical psychological malignancies.

Zak argues that the role of oxytocin in pro-social, normative human behavior and its inhibition in psychopaths may provide a further argument against culpability. He has coined a diagnostic designation to describe this chemical deficiency: Oxytocin Deficit Disorder (ODD). In psychopaths (who lack an emotional framework), could this chemical deficiency represent a crucial key to understanding psychopathy? Could it even provide a legal defense for psychopaths in criminal justice proceedings?

Neurobiology and psychopathy

Dr. James R. Blair's editorial in the British Journal of Psychiatry, published in January 2003, forms part of an impressive body of work produced by Blair on the link between neurobiology and psychopathy.

His Editorial, entitled Neurobiological basis of psychopathy, Dr. Blair explores the neurological origins of the disorder, decisively insisting that these are fundamental to understanding it. What's not understood, according to Blair, is why the neural systems involved are, indeed, dysfunctional. Also cited by Blair is evidence obtained through associated research that the frontal cortex may play a supporting role in the amygdala's dysfunction.

Blair again points out the central role of the amygdala (which plays a pivotal role in the recognition of facial expressions resulting from emotional responses). Dysfunction in this area of the brain (as discussed in the section on genetics and the brain earlier in this book) are important to the understanding of the psychopath's failure to read these expressions as emotional clues. They can't, because their brains are not equipped to. While the entire structure of this section of the brain was not found to be at fault, the section known as the orbitofrontal cortex (OFC) displayed possible impairment during the course of research, which correlates to its suspected impairment in the brains of psychopaths.

At the same time, Blair points out that lifestyle factors (the substance abuse often associated with psychopathic personalities) may impact brain function in the areas noted and that this should be taken into account. In other words, neurological impairment seen in subjects with this profile may not be entirely organic, but behaviorally induced.

Blair's study concludes that while dysfunction in the regions of the brain noted above are certainly implicated in psychopathy, it's not clear where the dysfunction originates. Without doubt, though, his research demonstrates that impairment in the brain is strong contributing factor to psychopathy.

Is there a "psycho gene"?

Research in this area has largely been conducted on sets of twins, both fraternal and identical. As stated earlier in this book, nature and nurture are considered equal partners by most in terms of their contributions to human personality. Where psychopathy is concerned, though, it's clear that research cited in this section indicates that biological and neurological origins are primary in the development of psychopathy.

In James Fallon's book, *The Psychopath inside: A Neuroscientist's Personal Journey into the Dark Side of the Brain*, Fallon details a shocking, personal discovery – that he has the brain of a psychopath.

Fallon not only discovered that he shared a brain with psychopaths, but that his family had a rather alarming history. His investigations in the wake of the revelation about the nature of his brain led him on a genetic journey that unearthed the presence of numerous murderers in his family background.

A successful neuroscientist with a happy family (including three children), Fallon's efforts to understand the apparent anomaly he represented in the world of psychopathy have opened the debate about genetics and their role in psychopathy even wider. Fallon has based his career on the study of psychopaths since the 1990s. Discovering that he was one of them; a man with a clinical background in psychopathy has provided a new, personalized lens for the scientific community to look through.

Fallon's next discovery, that there is a human gene that can be directly linked to psychopathy is the most notable for the purposes of this book. MAO-A (monoamine oxidase A). This gene has been seen to break down proteins responsible to the transmission of chemical "messengers" in our brains. The gene has been linked to aggression and violence in those who have it (thus the "psycho gene").

In his report, The Psycho Gene, Philip Hunter makes the link between MAO-A and its role in psychopathy. Hunter's preamble acknowledges that linking socially aberrant, asocial or anti-social behavior to genetics may have legal implications and this is, at least in part, the reason for the controversial nature of establishing a link between genetics and psychopathy.

Hunter points out that, in 2009, an Italian appeal court cut short the sentence of a convicted murderer, due to his defense – that the MOA-A gene was part of his genetic makeup and that he could not, therefore, be held legally accountable for his actions.

On the other side of the Atlantic, a different approach to a genetic basis for psychopathy is taken. Courts in the USA have tended to side with the prosecution in such instances, handing down stiffer sentences to those whose genetic makeup can be shown to indicate a tendency to violent behavior, or psychopathy. The grounds involved are that the fact these tendencies are rooted in genetics signals the perpetrator has no hope of reform.

Ultimately, Hunter arrives at the conclusion that genes do not dictate the behavior of the individual, but that free and the ability of the individual to think lucidly and in a pre-meditated fashion is the true determinate of culpability.

Summation

The preceding arguments are complex and compelling, still, it's questionable how far society can go to accommodate psychopaths in terms of their genetic makeup, chemical imbalances and dysfunction in the brain.

Following Hunter, who appears to reject any argument from biology, chemistry and neurology, psychopaths are entirely responsible for their actions due to their decision-making abilities. Just because an individual is pre-disposed to certain behaviors, in other words, is not to say that they are pre-*destined* to indulge in them.

So what do we do with them? Lock them up and throw away the key?

Continue to host them in our midst as they operate with impunity?

Is American jurisprudence, which argues that the genetic makeup associated with psychopathy demands stiffer sentences, correct?

Or are the Italian courts, which showed leniency, based on the same factor, correct?

As medical science and the psychiatric, psychological and philosophical disciplines continue to examine these questions, it's hoped that answers will become clear. For now, though, the issue of culpability remains a legal matter and a societal problem.

CHAPTER 15: LIFE AFTER A PSCYHOPATH

Healing: The Road to Recovery

Victims of psychopaths undergo immense trauma. The recovery process is often a slow and painful one. Former targets sometimes succumb to bouts of depression and are unable to trust or love other people, moving forward, due to the abuse they've suffered at the hands of a psychopath.

Psychopaths are petty and shallow. Matters you and I view as inconsequential are precisely those that attract the psychopath's attention. It's their level and it's not your fault.

If you're in a relationship with a psychopath, leave. Get out of the relationship and strike out in search of the better life you deserve. Seek the counsel and expert help of a therapist. There is no cure for psychopathy – but you are gifted with a saner view of the world. Seek ways and means to fill your life with the calm, order and sanity you crave and deserve.

Survivors of psychopathic abuse often find themselves frustrated because their healing takes longer than they and those around them had expected. The duration of recovery can lead to friends demanding that you "snap out of it" or "get over it", when in fact what victims need is time and understanding.

Ignore those who expect you to bounce back like a rubber bank. Take the time you need to heal.

Whether you were in a marriage or other romantic relationship or involved in a short affair, the impact of this experience can't be taken lightly. The recovery process will take time.

Be attentive to your feelings. Keep a journal detailing these. You may find it helps. Permit yourself to go through the full spectrum of the grieving process. While change it ultimately good, change you precipitated by unhealthy circumstances (especially relationships) can be difficult to absorb. Know that in letting something go, that by releasing it from your life, there's been a death. This is a profound change for you and acknowledging that change in terms of grieving is entirely appropriate.

Be open to recognizing the <u>stages of grief</u> as you move through them, taking care to take note of your emotions and their source as objectively as you can. This will help you take charge of them and in so doing, walk into the new life you've chosen whole and healthy.

What you've experienced amounts to trauma and many former targets of psychopaths suffered from Post-Traumatic Stress Disorder (PTSD). This condition haunts those who have been abused, witnessed violence (especially children, witnessing domestic violence), have been impacted by civil insurrection and war, or have experienced profound psychological shock or disturbance. If you recognize any of the following symptoms, you may be suffering from PTSD. It's important that you honestly assess yourself against these symptoms:

➢ Replaying events from the course of your relationship with the psychopath.

➢ Sudden flashbacks (not just replay; vivid and real).

➢ Sleep disturbances caused by nightmares based on events in the relationship.

➢ Distress at being reminded about any of these events.

If you have a combination of two or more of these symptoms, seek the help of a professional in overcoming the effects of this debilitating disorder. PTSD can lead to depression in those who suffer from it. Act to avoid complicating your mental health with another problem as soon as you're able.

The most important thing you can do is to stop blaming yourself. Resist the urge to indulge in the "what ifs" and "I should haves". None of this was your fault. You were the target of someone with a profound, incurable personality disorder. Sometimes we make choices we shouldn't. That's part of life. Learn what you can from the experience and move on.

Give yourself just as much or more time to work out the effects of the toxicity on your emotional and spiritual systems. Also, the avenues for finding help with your recovering in the Resources section, at the end of this book.

CONCLUSION

We hope this instructional book has given you a deeper understanding of psychopathy and its nature. While not written by a clinical professional, the book is informed by a variety of source materials, including those produced by experts in the field of the study and research of psychopathy. Care has been taken to present as clear and accurate a depiction of the pathology as possible.

As with any medical, psychological or psychiatric condition, it's of utmost importance that self-diagnosis, or the non-accredited diagnosis of others not be pursued. Only a medical professional can make a diagnosis of psychopathy.

If you suspect that you or someone you know or love is exhibiting the traits of psychopathy, consult a professional at your earliest opportunity. While it's true that you can manage some of the psychopath's behavior, it's not true that you can or should attempt to deal with this person on your own.

It's rare for psychopaths to be aware or consider the possibility they suffer from this disorder. This can make it difficult to obtain a diagnosis. That doesn't prevent you, as someone who's been affected or is being affected by the actions of a psychopath to pro-actively look for solutions. The best way to do that is to consult your family doctor for a referral to a specialist familiar with the disorder.

Psychopaths and the havoc they wreak in the lives of others and even the world as a whole are a problem that's not going away any time soon. While there is no cure for psychopathy, the findings of some of the studies cited in this book clearly indicate that there is hope of an eventual solution to the damage caused by the disorder and those who suffer from it. The human, financial and societal costs of psychopathy demand that research continue to be vigorously pursued.

We join you in the hope of a psychopath free world and that this hope is realized in the not too distant future.

In the meantime – be aware of this shadow on the human soul – psychopathy.

YOU MAY ENJOY SOME OF MY OTHER BOOKS

Author Page

http://hyperurl.co/Jeffdawson

NARCISSISM: Self Centered Narcissistic Personality Exposed

hyperurl.co/narc

Personality Disorders: Histronic and Borderline Personality Disorders Unmasked

hyperurl.co/borderline

BODY LANGUAGE: How To Spot A Liar And Communicate Clearly

hyperurl.co/bodylang

Boundaries In Marriage: Line Between Right And Wrong

hyperurl.co/marriage

<u>Boundaries: Crossing The Line:</u> Workplace Success and Office Sex

hyperurl.co/crossline

<u>Personality Disorders:</u> Psychopath or Narcissistic Lover?

hyperurl.co/psy

RESOURCES

The Psychopathy Checklist:
http://vistriai.com/psychopathtest/

Without Conscience: http://www.amazon.com/Without-Conscience-Disturbing-World-Psychopaths/dp/1572304510

Dr. Robert D. Hare's website: http://www.hare.org/

The Mask of Sanity: http://www.amazon.com/The-Mask-Sanity-Psychopathic-Personality/dp/0962151904

The Pscyhopathy Self-Report Scale: http://personality-testing.info/tests/LSRP.php

Snakes in Suits: http://www.amazon.com/Snakes-Suits-When-Psychopaths-Work/dp/0061147893

The Corporation: http://www.thecorporation.com/

Aftermath: Surviving Psychopathy: http://aftermath-surviving-psychopathy.org/

Psychopath Victims: http://psychopathvictims.com/

Post-Traumatic Stress Disorder Association:
http://www.ptsdassociation.com/

Gift From Within

End note and Disclaimer: The writer is not a licensed doctor. Any and all questions and inquiries should be directed to a licensed clinician before resorting to clinical trials or research studies. Receiving a valid, professional diagnosis is indispensable for safety reasons.

Printed in Great Britain
by Amazon

29209704R00076